POWER WRITING

Writing
with a Purpose

ADULT BASIC EDUCATION
NORTHWEST TECHNICAL COLLEGE
WADENA, MN 56482
1-800-247-2007

CAMBRIDGE ADULT EDUCATION

A Division of Simon & Schuster

Upper Saddle River, New Jersey

Executive Editor: Mark Moscowitz

Project Editors: Karen Bernhaut, Douglas Falk, Amy Jolin, Kristen Shepos-Salvatore

Series Editor: Michael Buchman

Development Editor: Mary McGarry

Writers: Roberta Moore, Linda Stern, Betsy Feist

Production Editor: Alan Dalgleish

Art Director: Pat Smythe

Interior Design and Electronic Page Production: Margarita Giammanco

Marketing Manager: Will Jarred

Cover Design: Sheree Goodman Designs

Printed in the United States of America

1 2 3 4 5 6 7 8 9 10   99 98 97 96 95

ISBN 0-8359-4667-3

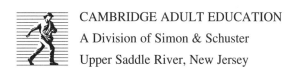

CAMBRIDGE ADULT EDUCATION

A Division of Simon & Schuster

Upper Saddle River, New Jersey

Contents

What is Power Writing?

Power Writing is a series of four books that help you build your writing skills. Every chapter begins with a real-life situation involving people you might find in your neighborhood. The skills you learn in the lessons and exercises will begin your preparation for the Graduate Equivalency Degree (GED) Writing Test. Each chapter ends with writing assignments that apply the skills from the lessons and relate to the life skills introduced at the beginning of the chapter.

The first two books help strengthen your grammatical knowledge and sentence-writing skills. You will develop an editing checklist, and you will begin using the techniques of the writing process to build a portfolio.

The last two books focus on the writing process and help you write more effective paragraphs and essays. You will also review grammatical skills as you revise and edit the work in your growing portfolio.

The contents of each book shows the skills presented. These skills were carefully selected and coordinated with the Test of Adult Basic Education (TABE). The Life Skill themes are based on the Comprehensive Adult Student Assessment System (CASAS).

How do you get started? Identify the appropriate book for your skill level by taking the Locator Test found in the Instructor's Guide. You may choose to review material that you already know. In each chapter you will:

- Read the opening story and study the Key Terms and Life Skill Words.
- Complete short lessons and exercises.
- Work on writing assignments designed to:
  – Build your vocabulary and use the glossary.
  – Read and write about related ideas.
  – Establish a writing portfolio.

Use the Answer Key at the back of each book to check your work after you have completed all the questions in an exercise. Ask your instructor to explain any answer you don't understand.

The Writing Process

Good writers take risks. Good writers are rewriters. Good writers become good editors. Through the activities in these books you will progress through clear stages: prewriting and idea generation, drafting, revising, editing, and publishing.

Good writers also know that writing is thinking. As you develop your ideas you will move back and forward through the writing process until your thoughts are clearly communicated.

As you work through each book in this series you will see your power to communicate grow. This power will help you in your daily life and in your continuing education.

Chapter 1

Writing with a Purpose

Mohammed Jones and his best friend, Tom Brown, had just landed jobs on the crew of a building contractor. The job would be an easy commute from their apartment in Detroit.

When they were hired, they were given a list of clothes needed before they could start. They would have to buy a tool belt, heavy-duty work pants, work gloves, and steel-toed work boots.

"I have no idea where to shop for this stuff," said Mohammed. "Maybe my big sister, Shantell, can help. She's got a job on the assembly line at Carter's, and she's always helped me shop."

"Shantell? Are you kidding? She'll have you looking at no-name discount stuff," said Tom scornfully. "This is our first job, and we need to make a good impression. I'm going to the mall, and I'm going for top-name brands and top quality!"

Mohammed scoffed at his friend, "I'd prefer a bargain any day!"

Key Terms

- audience
- descriptive
- dictionary
- drafting
- editing
- informative
- narrative
- paragraph
- persuasive
- prewriting
- publishing
- purpose
- revising
- thesaurus
- topic
- topic sentence
- writing plan
- writing process

Life Skill Words

- dry cleaning
- fad
- returns
- run
- seams
- synthetic material
- wardrobe
- workmanship

 **Lesson 1**

Identifying Your Topic and Purpose

A **topic** is the subject you are writing about. A topic might be *applying for a job, my job interview, shopping for clothes,* or *dressing for success.* Having a specific topic can help you focus your ideas.

Your **purpose** in writing is related to your topic. There are four basic purposes in writing:

1. Writing that tells a story or lists events is **narrative** in purpose.

2. Writing that describes the physical aspects of something or someone is **descriptive.**

3. When you explain something, or provide unbiased information, your purpose is to be **informative.**

4. When you give your point of view or try to change your reader's mind, your purpose is to be **persuasive.**

Exercise 1.1

Read each paragraph and identify the topic and the writer's purpose. An example is done for you.

Example: To get to the Sears store, take Route 135 South and turn right on Jackson Road. At the third traffic light you will see a Mobil gas station. Turn left onto Bellvue Street and follow it to the end. The Sears store will be on your right.

> *Topic:*   <u>How to get to the Sears store</u>

> *Writer's Purpose:*   <u>Informative</u>

1. In my opinion, if you want to succeed on the job, you should dress like your boss. People will unconsciously see you supporting your superior if you adopt the same style. Your boss will be flattered that you admire his or her appearance. He or she may even compliment you on your good taste! I think that although "dressing right" is no substitute for good work, making the right impression can only help you.

Topic: _____

Writer's Purpose: _____

2. You may not think so but it's important to check the care instructions on an item of clothing before you buy it. Some clothing will require **dry cleaning,** which can be expensive. Some colored clothing must be washed separately because the color may **run** and stain your other clothes. Other clothing may be ruined in hot water or high-temperature drying. Be careful! Before you add an item to your **wardrobe,** be sure you are prepared to care for it.

    Topic: _____

    Writer's Purpose: _____

3. When I entered the Men's Work Clothes department, I heard a familiar voice addressing the clerk. His back was to me, but I recognized my new boss immediately. I ducked behind a rack of winter jackets and listened carefully. I felt like a fool, but I felt too embarrassed to say hello.

    Topic: _____

    Writer's Purpose: _____

4. The shoes were just what I was looking for. The soles were a thick nonskid material, which is good because we sometimes work in the rain. The heavy steel toe was essential to protect me from accidentally dropped equipment. Best of all, they looked like nice black dress shoes and took a good shine when polished.

    Topic: _____

    Writer's Purpose: _____

5. The prices of these shoes are influenced by the materials the shoes are made of and the **workmanship** of the manufacturer. The more expensive pair has leather uppers and a replaceable *Vibram* sole. The cheaper pair is made of entirely **synthetic** (sihn-THEHT-ihk) **material,** and its sole cannot be replaced. The **seams** of the expensive shoes are double stitched while the others have welded seams.

    Topic: _____

    Writer's Purpose: _____

6. Anyone can learn to select a comfortable shoe. The trick is to focus on the fit. Wear the kind of socks or stockings you expect to wear with the shoe. Select a size according to your measurement. Since different manufacturers size their shoes differently, try on the pair. Be sure to lace or buckle the shoe securely. You should have a thumb's width of space at your toe, and the sides should be neither too loose nor too tight. Finally, walk around in the shoes. If you are unsure about the fit, ask the clerk about the store's policy on **returns.**

Topic: _____

Writer's Purpose: _____

Check your answers on page 120.

Considering Your Audience

How you treat your topic depends on your **audience,** or expected readers. You might not tell a joke to your mother the same way as you might tell it to your friends in a bowling alley. Your choice of words may differ, depending on whom you are addressing.

Depending on your audience, you may choose a formal or informal style. You also will choose a format to match your purpose. For example, a business letter will look and sound different from a note to a friend.

Furthermore, decide what **outcome,** or result, you expect from your writing. *What should your readers do or feel?* If you state your intended outcome clearly, you can sharpen your topic and purpose. You can select details to meet your goal.

You should write down your topic, audience, purpose, style, and intended outcomes to start a **writing plan.** (Your plan will also include an *outline,* which we will discuss in Chapter 2.)

The following writing plan is unfinished. Think about the different details the writer might include to achieve the possible outcomes.

Topic:	Clothes shopping
Audience:	A sister or brother
Purpose:	Narrative
Style:	Informal

Possible Intended Outcomes
>   *Reader's Feelings:* surprise? pride? amusement? sympathy? outrage at the store?
>   *Reader's Actions:*   a return letter? a return phone call? an angry letter to the store?

Obviously, the reader's feelings and actions will depend on what the writer says and how he or she says it. The reader might start out thinking that the writer had no fashion sense. A description of the successful selection of several outfits might inspire surprise and pride.

On the other hand, a story of a series of problems might inspire sympathy. Depending on how it was told, the reader might feel amused by the situation, thinking, "Only you could have such luck!" Alternatively, the writer might present details to make the reader feel angry at the store.

While you do not control your reader's reaction, your writing will have influence. If you want your reader to take a specific action, you should probably suggest it.

Exercise 1.2a

Create a writing plan for the four pairs of topics and audiences that are given below. For each set, decide if your style should be formal or informal. Then suggest a purpose and one or more outcomes that could result from something you might write. An example is done for you.

Example:

Topic:	Clothing sales at Smith's Department Store
Audience:	A friend
Style:	formal / (informal)

Purpose: _persuasive_

Outcome(s): _envy at the great sales at my local store; a visit for a shopping trip_

1.

Topic:	How to wash baby clothes
Audience:	A child care class
Style:	formal / informal

Purpose: _____

Outcome(s): _____

2.

Topic:	My favorite dry cleaner
Audience:	The local chamber of commerce (an organization of business owners)
Style:	formal / informal

Purpose: _____

Outcome(s): _____

3. Topic: My favorite shoes
   Audience: A friend
   Style: formal / informal

   Purpose: _____

   Outcome(s): _____

4. Topic: Our last tag sale
   Audience: Church newsletter
   Style: formal / informal

   Purpose: _____

   Outcome(s): _____

Check your answers on page 120.

Exercise 1.2b

Choose one of the topics from Exercise 1.2a. In the space below, list at least three details you might include to achieve the purpose and outcomes you suggested. An example is done for you.

Example: Topic: <u>Clothing sales at Smith's Department Store</u>
           Details: <u>the prices and selection at last spring's sporting</u>
                     <u>goods sale; what I bought at the Mother's Day sale;</u>
                     <u>the upcoming work clothes clearance blowout</u>

Topic: _____

Details: _____

_____

_____

Check your answers on page 120.

Writing Beyond One Paragraph

A **paragraph** contains one or more sentences on a single topic. Often, a paragraph contains a **topic sentence** that states the main idea. When you need to write in detail about several related ideas however, you may need to write a series of paragraphs.

Some paragraphs are complete in themselves. Others do not explain the topic sentence completely. They call out for more development; the reader has more questions and wants more details to support the ideas presented.

Exercise 1.3a

The following paragraph can be broken into three. Mark an *X* before each sentence that should begin a new paragraph. Then underline the topic sentence in each of the three paragraphs.

> You might be tempted to write one very long paragraph. Breaking your thoughts into several smaller parts, however, has advantages for both you and your reader. Using short paragraphs makes the writer's job easier. Short paragraphs let you easily check that you covered each idea thoroughly. You will notice if you are mixing ideas together, or if you are leaving out something important. Short paragraphs are also easier to understand. Your readers will be able to concentrate on one idea at a time. They will also know that you intend a new idea to begin with each bite-sized paragraph.

Check your answers on page 120.

Exercise 1.3b

Read each of the following paragraphs. The following paragraphs do not develop their topic sentences fully. Write some questions telling the writer what to explain. An example is done for you.

Example: I don't buy fancy athletic shoes. The thugs in my neighborhood might try to steal them, and the overpriced shoes aren't really much better than ordinary sneakers, anyway.

More: Why do thugs steal shoes? In what way are the expensive shoes the same as other shoes? Are there any differences? Why do people want them so much?

1. I prefer a winter jacket filled with synthetic fiber to one filled with down. Some feathers always leak out of the shell, and I think my wife is allergic to them. She never sneezes around Thinsulate®!

_____

_____

_____

2. I always sort my wash into whites, colors, and delicates. They come out better when they are washed separately, because you wash them differently.

_____

_____

_____

3. Shantell went shopping with her friend Liza, who was about to be married. Shantell had had a lousy day. Her coworkers blamed her for shutting down the assembly line, and she thought her boss agreed, although he did not exactly say so. "Maybe I'll buy a new dress to cheer myself up," she thought aloud.

_____

_____

_____

4. Tom always likes to wear the latest styles. He buys lots of fad clothing, things that are very popular for a very short while. His closets are full of things he would be embarrassed to wear today. Mohammed has tried to convince Tom to stick to styles that last. Tom just can't seem to help himself, though.

_____

_____

_____

Check your answers on page 120.

The Writing Process

Whether you are writing one paragraph or an entire book, you can do the job more easily if you break it down into smaller parts. Your aim is to get your ideas down on paper in a way that your readers will understand.

The **writing process** is a series of five steps that lead to a finished written work. This book is organized according to the writing process.

1. The **prewriting** stage is the time you gather ideas and create a writing plan. You might use the library, interviews, or your own thoughts. Chapters 1 and 2 mostly deal with prewriting.

2. The **drafting** stage is your chance to get ideas down quickly, without worrying about grammar, spelling, or details. Chapter 3 presents this stage and Chapters 4 through 9 present techniques for drafting according to different purposes.

3. The **revising** stage is your chance to rethink your work. You can add or cut ideas and details. You can change the order that you present things. You can also rewrite sentences and paragraphs to be more clear and effective. Chapters 10 and 11 present techniques for revision.

4. The **editing** stage is when you polish your work. You double-check spelling, capitalization, and grammar. Chapter 12 discusses ideas for successful editing.

5. The **publishing** stage is when you make your writing "public." You share it with others. In this course you will "publish" every time you share your work with your instructor, your fellow students, or your friends and family. Good writers often seek the reactions of trusted readers. The ideas their readers offer may lead to another revision and an improved work.

Writing essays, reports, business letters, and stories may seem difficult at first. When you break the job into steps, though, you can get it done. Your skills and knowledge will increase, and you will surprise yourself as your imagination takes form in writing.

Exercise 1.4

Read the list of writing activities below. In the space provided, identify the stage of the writing process that best fits the activity: *prewriting, drafting, revising, editing,* or *publishing*. An example is done for you.

Example: __editing__ Check punctuation.

1. _____ Rearrange your paragraphs.

2. _____ Correct grammatical errors.

3. _____ Ask someone to read what you wrote.

4. _____ Think about what to write.

5. _____ Take notes on a topic from a magazine article.

6. _____ Make your writing clearer.

7. _____ Get ideas on paper quickly and completely.

8. _____ List your purpose, audience, and expected outcomes.

9. _____ Put your information in readable form.

10. _____ Check spelling.

Check your answers on page 120.

IN OTHER WORDS, LOOK IT UP!

At times you will want a different way of expressing an idea. Maybe you have used the same word or phrase too often. Or you might get stuck, not knowing exactly what you mean. Two books can help you out of a word jam: a dictionary and a thesaurus.

Using a Dictionary

As you know, a **dictionary** is an alphabetical list of words. For each word you will find a pronunciation and definition. Many words have several meanings. Some words have *synonyms* (words with similar meanings) or *antonyms* (opposites). Dictionaries sometimes suggest that you compare one word with another to see the similarities and differences in meaning.

When you look up a word in a dictionary, you can save time by using the *guide words* at the top of each page. These represent the first and last words on that page. If the word you want falls between the guide words, you know you are on the right page!

Using a Thesaurus

A **thesaurus** (thih-SAWR-uhs) is a book of words and their synonyms. A thesaurus also includes phrases and expressions that have similar meanings. The words are grouped in categories in the front of the book. You look up a word by using the index at the back of book.

The index is an alphabetical listing of words. Beside each word is a number. This number stands for the category (*not* the page number) where you will find the word. Find the category number at the top of the page in the first part of the thesaurus. Then you can read a list of similar meanings and expressions.

In the index some words, like *wardrobe* or *run*, have more than one category number. Each stands for a different meaning. Some words have synonyms listed in the index, each with its own category number.

If you are ever out of ideas or ways to express them, try a dictionary or thesaurus. In other words, look it up!

Writing Assignments

Building Your Word Power

Start a word notebook. Include the Key Terms and Life Skill Words from this chapter. Break each word into syllables. Write an original sentence for at least five of the words. Then choose a few of the words and write synonyms for them.

You may use the glossary in the back of this book. You may also check a dictionary to read about other uses and meanings of these words. Finally, you may use a thesaurus, a book of synonyms.

Reading to Write

Clip or photocopy a page from a clothing catalog or an article on clothing or clothing care from a consumer magazine. Add three words from this article to your word notebook.

Writer's Portfolio Assignment

Start a writer's portfolio. Use a notebook or folder to store the ideas you collect and the writing you produce. To start, list the different audiences you might write for. Then think of at least one topic for each audience. For each topic add some possible purposes and the outcomes you might expect. You can organize your ideas in a chart like the one below.

Audiences	Topics	Purposes	Expected Outcomes
my grandmother	why folks wear caps backward	informative	better understanding of young people

Chapter 2

Prewriting: Generating Ideas and Outlining

"Tom," said Mohammed, "I've been thinking. Those clothes we bought at Sears were good **quality,** but I'm not sure we got the best price."

"What do you mean?" asked Tom.

"Well, I saw in yesterday's newspaper that the Kmart out on Twelve Mile Road had sneakers for almost two dollars less than what we paid for ours."

"No kidding?" Tom shook his head.

"I guess we should have done some **comparison shopping,**" said Mohammed.

"What do you mean?" Tom asked. Do you really want to run all over town to save a couple of bucks?"

"By the time we add up everything we bought, it could be more than a couple of bucks," said Mohammed.

"Yea?" Tom looked disgusted. "As far as I'm concerned all stores are **overpriced.** There's no point in running all over town looking for a bargain. I just buy what I want, when I have the money."

"That's dangerous. Think of it this way—it's worth the effort, and in the end you can have more—more clothes and more money!"

Key Terms

- brainstorm
- cluster map
- conclusion
- introduction
- outline
- thesis statement

Life Skill Words

- comparison shopping
- overpriced
- quality

Editing a Brainstormed List

When you use the writing process, you develop your work in stages. In each stage, you have a chance to think about, write down, add, take out, and change your ideas. Prewriting is when you generate ideas and get them organized.

Once you know your topic, audience, and purpose, ask yourself, "What do I want to say?" Your mind may be full of ideas or it may be a complete blank. Whatever the case, your writing should not begin until after you have generated and thought about your ideas.

One way to generate ideas to work with is to **brainstorm.** To brainstorm, means to let your ideas flow freely. As ideas come into your head, write them down in a list. Try not to think about whether the ideas are good or not. Don't even worry about whether they fit the topic well. Don't try to write complete sentences or put anything in order. Just write whatever comes into your mind. Write as many ideas as you can for a short period of time. Reread your list. Let your words spark new ideas.

Once your list is complete, you can revise and edit it. You can add or change ideas or get rid of the ones you don't want. Just cross off the ideas you don't want and add what might be missing. Then circle the main ideas on your list. The main ideas are the most important ideas on the list. They are the ones you can expand when you begin to write. If any other ideas are left, you can put them aside and decide if you want to use them later.

Exercise 2.1a

On a separate sheet of paper brainstorm a list of ideas for each topic listed below or another topic of your choice. Remember to write whatever comes into your mind. Don't take time to write in complete sentences. An example is done for you.

Example: Topic: Dressing for work on a small budget
List: dress up or casual
kind of clothes for job
how much to spend
basics
necessities
what you already have
fix up old clothes
borrow things

1. Topic: How to be a smart clothes shopper
2. Topic: A bad buying decision I made
3. Topic: Which is more important—quality or quantity of clothes?

Now edit your brainstormed lists. Circle the main ideas. Cross off ideas that don't fit the topic, repeated ideas, weak ideas.

Example: Topic: Dressing for work on a small budget

Brainstormed List: dress up or casual

⟨kind of clothes for job⟩

how much to spend

⟨basics⟩

⟨necessities⟩

⟨what you already have⟩

~~fix up old clothes~~

~~borrow things~~

Cluster Mapping

When you are satisfied with your brainstormed list, you can begin to organize it. A good way to organize ideas is to create a cluster map. A **cluster map** is a visual way to look at your ideas and relate them to each other. To create a cluster map, begin with your general topic. Write it down in the middle of a blank sheet of paper and draw a circle around it. Next, draw lines around the circle like the spokes of a wheel. At the end of each spoke, write one of the main ideas from your brainstormed list. These circles should contain ideas that are most important to the development of your topic.

Each circle can become a cluster of ideas if you want to add to it. Draw spokes and write additional related ideas. When your map is finished, you may want to cross out some clusters and keep others. Remember, this is a work in progress. You can redraw the entire map as many times as you like to get the ideas to work together.

Here is an example of a cluster map for the topic: Dressing for work on a small budget.

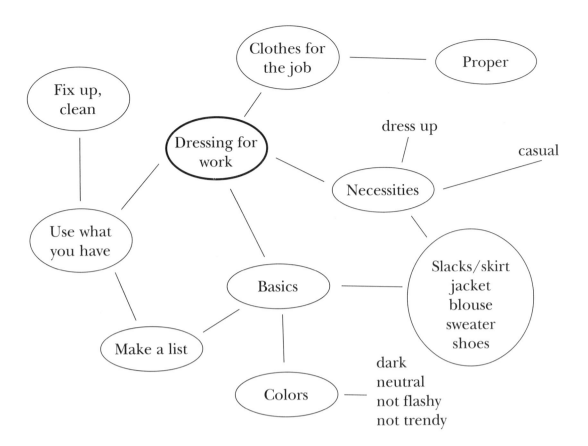

Exercise 2.2

Choose one of the brainstormed lists you wrote in Exercise 2.1 and develop a cluster map in the space below.

Writing a Thesis Statement

Your cluster map is the first step in organizing your ideas. Before continuing to organize, you need to make a decision about your topic. A **thesis statement** expresses your opinion or point of view about a topic. It introduces your topic in one sentence and tells what you want the reader to know about your topic. Once you have written your thesis statement, you will then support it using the ideas you have written down.

For example, if your topic is "Returning damaged goods to the store," what is your point of view about this topic? A thesis statement for this topic might be:

> Don't take "no" for an answer when you need to return damaged goods to the store.

Often your thesis statement can be used as the opening sentence of your piece. However, it doesn't have to be. It can just be the central idea that you have in your mind as you begin to develop what you want to say.

Exercise 2.3a

Write a thesis statement for the cluster map you created in Exercise 2.2. An example is done for you.

Example   Topic: Dressing for work on a small budget
            Thesis: To dress well for work you don't need a closet
                     full of designer clothes.

Topic: _____

Thesis Statement: _____

_____

Exercise 2.3b

On a separate sheet of paper draw a cluster map for your two remaining brainstorm lists written in Exercise 2.1. Then, use the space below to write topics and thesis statements for each list.

1. Topic: _____

   Thesis Statement: _____

2. Topic: _____

Thesis Statement: _____

_____

Outlining

Your thesis statement focuses on the general point that you want to get across to your reader. Before you write a draft, you should outline your ideas to support this thesis. An **outline** is an organized list of ideas that shows how the ideas are related to each other.

When you get ready to outline, look for groups of related ideas in your cluster map. Name these groups of ideas and make them the main ideas in your outline. You may decide not to use all the idea groups in your cluster map. You may feel some ideas are not important enough. Other ideas may take you away from the topic. Make sure the ideas you end up with cover the topic completely, though.

To write your outline, decide what is the most logical order for presenting your ideas. If you are writing a narrative piece, you will probably want to organize your ideas in time order. If you are writing a persuasive piece, you may want to organize your ideas in order of importance, time, comparison, or cause and effect. You will learn more about how to order your ideas for specific kinds of writing in Chapter 4.

The example below includes the main ideas from the cluster map on page 15. Ideas in the upper right of that map are covered by "Proper clothes for the job." Ideas in the lower right of the map are covered by "Basics and necessities." Ideas in the left side of the map are covered by "Use what you have." Notice the thesis statement grew from the central idea in the cluster map. Writers often find that their point of view develops after they have worked with some of the details.

> ### *Example:*
> **Thesis Statement:** To dress well for work you don't need a closet full of designer clothes.
>
> I. Introduction
> II. Proper clothes for the job
> III. Basics and necessities
> IV. Use what you have
> V. Conclusion

Use Roman numerals for the main headings in an outline. Later, you will use Arabic numerals and letters to fill in the rest of the outline. This system helps you see at a glance the relationships of all the ideas in your final outline.

Notice that the outline includes an introduction and a conclusion. These two items will be included in every piece you write. The **introduction** gives your thesis statement and explains it to the reader. The **conclusion** restates the thesis, ties the ideas together, and leaves the reader with a parting thought. Including them in your outline will help you to always remember to write them.

Exercise 2.4

1. Write the main headings of an outline for a piece, based on the cluster map below.

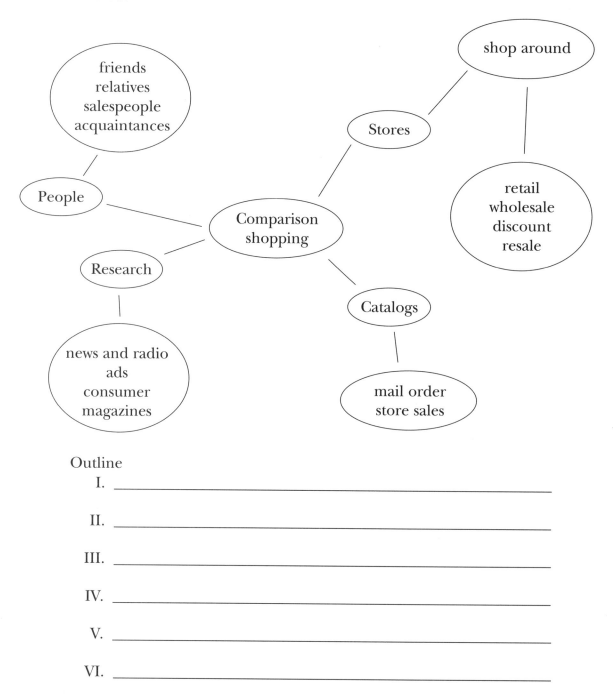

Outline

I. _____

II. _____

III. _____

IV. _____

V. _____

VI. _____

2. Write the thesis statement and the main headings of an outline, using one of the cluster maps you have developed.

Thesis Statement: _____

_____

Outline: _____

_____

_____

_____

_____

_____

_____

Check your answers on page 121.

Lesson 5

Adding Details to Your Outline

The main ideas in your outline are the framework for the piece you will write. Before you begin filling in the details of your outline, you should know how long a piece you are going to write. This will help you plan how many paragraphs you will need for each heading. In a short piece, each main heading may be one paragraph. In a longer piece, you may write two or three paragraphs under each heading.

To complete your outline, rewrite each main heading and place the related ideas under the main headings. Your ideas may come from your cluster map. You may also think of other ideas to make your point.

As you look at each word or phrase remaining on your cluster map, decide if it is a supporting idea or detail. A supporting idea is something that is necessary to understanding the main idea. If you are telling a narrative in time order, a supporting idea would be what happened within a certain time period. Indent your supporting ideas in your outline under the main ideas and label them A, B, C, and so on.

A detail explains something about a supporting idea, for example, how you felt about what happened or how someone else reacted to what happened. Indent details under supporting ideas and label them 1, 2, 3, and so on.

Here is the completed outline for the topic: Dressing for work on a small budget.

I. Introduction
   A. Thesis: You don't need designer clothes
      1. Look neat and well groomed
      2. Wear proper attire
II. Right clothes for the job
   A. Find out what's appropriate
      1. Casual
      2. Dress up
III. Basics and necessities
   A. Wear basic colors
      1. Dark and neutral
      2. Not flashy or trendy
   B. Wear basic styles
      1. Slacks/skirt
      2. Blouse/sweater
      3. Jacket and tie (maybe)
      4. Comfortable shoes
IV. Use what you have
   A. Look through closet
      1. Make a list
      2. Match up items
   B. Fix up and clean
      1. Sew or remodel
      2. Dry clean or wash
V. Conclusion

As you develop your complete outline, try not to feel locked into it. Are there ideas that would be better in a different order? Should something be added or taken out? Remember that this is a blueprint for your writing. The ideas in your outline should flow comfortably. Otherwise you may get stuck when you begin to write. Keep working with the outline until you feel that the ideas are in a logical order, that related ideas are together, and that your subject is covered as completely as necessary.

Exercise 2.5

Using your outline of main headings and your cluster map, write a complete outline on your chosen topic.

REVIEW: ELIMINATING DISTRACTING DETAILS

Avoid Distracting Details

You always want to make sure you tell the reader enough about your topic. On the other hand, you don't want to tell so much that the reader gets bored or loses track of your main point. Too many details can be distracting. They can draw attention away from the main point. Once you lose a reader's attention, you may never get it back. The person may stop reading or continue reading, but stop thinking about what your piece says. Have you ever listened while someone told you about an "interesting" experience in such detail that you almost fell asleep? Do you have a friend who calls you on the phone and tells you the details of his or her life whether or not you want to hear them? If so, then you know firsthand how deadly too many details can be.

When you brainstorm, map, and outline your ideas, edit them and eliminate distracting details. If you are unsure about including something, ask a friend or fellow student's advice. Something that may be interesting to you may be dull or off the point to someone else. Keeping an eye out for distracting details will improve your writing!

Sketching a Conclusion

The conclusion summarizes the main points of your piece. It comes at the end and is usually no longer than one paragraph. If you sketch a conclusion in your outline, you will have an idea of where you are headed. When you sketch your conclusion, you need to look at your main headings and make sure that you haven't brought in any new ideas. If you have, ask yourself why. Does something need to be added to your outline? Do you need to change your thesis statement? By knowing your conclusion before you write, you make sure that your whole piece will hang together and make sense to the reader.

Here is an example of the conclusion for the topic: Dressing for work on a tight budget.

Conclusion: A neat, basic wardrobe will work for most jobs. Buy only a few basics. Fix up, clean, and use what you have. Don't try to be high fashion or flashy.

Exercise 2.6

In the space below, sketch out your conclusion for the outline you developed.

_____

_____

_____

_____

Writing Assignments

Building Your Word Power

Write the Key Terms and Life Skill Words listed in the beginning of this chapter in your notebook. Break each word into syllables. Write an original sentence for at least five of the words. Then choose a few of the words and write synonyms for them.

You may use the glossary in the back of this book. You may also check a dictionary to read about other uses and meanings of these words. Finally, you may use a thesaurus, a book of synonyms.

Reading to Write

Clip or photocopy ads for clothing from your local newspaper or a catalog. Select ads that could be used to illustrate the piece you outlined. Add three words that describe these clothes to your notebook.

Building Your Portfolio

Write thesis statements and develop complete outlines for the two additional cluster maps you worked on in this chapter. Add them to your portfolio.

Chapter 3

Purposes and Organizing Principles

Gloria took the long bus ride home to visit her family for the holidays. She and Raul compared their **budgets** to see how much they could spend on gifts for their parents and their younger sister. "If we pool our money, we can buy more expensive gifts," said Gloria.

"You haven't changed," teased Raul, "You're as **thrifty** as ever."

"I have to be even more thrifty now that I don't live at home anymore," replied Gloria laughing. "I clip coupons, share an apartment, and I only eat out on very special occasions."

"I know what you mean," said Raul. "Now that I have to buy all my own clothes, I know where all the discount stores are. But I still don't know what happens to my paycheck. I make out a budget, but every week I end up borrowing before payday."

Gloria smiled. "All I can tell you is that making out a budget is only half the battle. Sticking to it is the real challenge. You've got to have willpower."

"You're right," Raul agreed. "I guess if you don't have a big bank account, willpower is the next best thing. But it's hard to resist buying things when they're all around you. When I see something I want, if I have some money, I just buy it."

Gloria shook her head. "That's **impulse buying**, Raul. That's the worst habit you can have. You've got to be strong. Ignore all the ads and store windows. Once you change your way of thinking, it gets easier."

"Sure," Raul nodded. "As soon as Christmas is over, that's what I'll do. Meanwhile, let's go to Hudson's. I want to look at a gift I saw in the paper. I know Mom would love it!"

Key Terms

- authority
- body paragraph
- introductory paragraph
- source

Life Skill Words

- brand name
- budget
- generic brand
- impulse buying
- thrifty

The Introductory Paragraph

No matter what you are writing, the first thing you want to do is get your reader's attention. You need to give your reader a reason to continue. The way to do this is to write a strong introductory paragraph. The **introductory paragraph** tells the reader what you are writing about and states the thesis of your piece. If the reader does not get interested or is turned off by the introduction, he or she may stop reading or not give full attention to the rest of the piece.

An effective introductory paragraph should do the following things:

1. Attract the reader's interest.
2. Present the thesis statement.
3. Give supporting ideas that explain what the piece is about.

There are several methods you can use when writing introductory paragraphs. The most common method is to begin with a general statement of your topic and narrow it down to your thesis statement. In the following paragraph, the writer talks generally about advertising and then makes a thesis statement about it:

> Everyday we are bombarded with advertisements that say to us, "Spend money!" Do you have a strong enough will to stay within your budget and buy only the things you need—not the things advertisers tell you to want?

In this example the writer attracts the reader's interest by calling attention to something that is familiar to the reader—advertising. The writer makes a general statement that readers can agree with. In the thesis statement, the writer challenges readers to think about their spending power. There is a good chance that the reader will want to find out what else the writer has to say.

Here are some common methods of writing introductory paragraphs. Select a method or a combination of methods that is right for your topic and the message you want to send to your reader.

1. *Make a general statement and then narrow it down with your thesis statement.* After presenting your thesis statement, support it with statements that introduce the main points you intend to cover in the rest of the piece.

> Advertisers want us to spend our money on their products. It is up to us as consumers to make good decisions about how we spend our money and which products we spend it on. Good buying decisions are based on living within your means on a budget. Buying decisions should be planned and consumers should take the time to make sure they are getting what they need for the best price.

2. *Ask one or more questions.* These questions may be answered in the reader's mind, or you may answer them as you develop your piece.

> Everyday we are bombarded with advertisements that say to us, "Spend money!" Do you have a strong enough will to stay within your budget and buy only the things you need—not the things advertisers tell you to want? Do you need the new Michael Jackson CD or can you listen to it on the radio? Do you have to have the **brand name** cereal to be healthy, or will the **generic brand** work just as well? The wise consumer knows the answers to these questions.

3. *Explain to the reader why your topic is important.* If you convince readers that your topic is important or interesting, they will want to continue reading.

> Sometimes, as a consumer, you may find it hard to resist the appeal of advertisers. Without a strong will, however, you may find yourself deeply in debt. Living within your budget and buying only the things you need, when you need them, is what makes you a smart consumer.

4. *Use an anecdote or brief story.* Most people are drawn in by a story of someone else's experiences. Stories paint a picture and make ideas come to life.

> My little boy is not a crier, but when I told him we couldn't afford the latest action figure hero, big crocodile tears formed in his eyes and flooded his chubby cheeks. How could I resist? The battle between television advertisers and my budget was lost once again.

5. *Make an opening statement that is the exact opposite of your thesis.* Stating two opposing ideas will surprise your readers and peak their interest.

> It feels great to blow your whole paycheck on something you want, whether you can afford it or not. Living within your budget and shopping wisely may not give you a thrill, but in the long run, you will thank yourself for being a wise consumer.

6. *Begin with a quotation.* You may quote a famous person, a proverb, or a saying that people are familiar with. Quotations can add support to your point of view and make the reader take notice.

> Many people are known for "being tight with a dollar" or "still having the first dollar they ever earned." We can all take a lesson from thrifty people when it comes to budgeting and buying. They have learned to close their ears to advertisers and buy only what they need at the best price available.

Exercise 3.1a

For each topic listed below write an introductory statement and thesis statement using the method given.

1. Topic: What makes a wise consumer

   Method: Make a general statement.

_____

_____

_____

_____

2. Topic: A purchase I regret

   Method: Ask questions.

_____

_____

_____

_____

3. Topic: The importance of reading labels

   Method: Explain importance.

_____

_____

_____

_____

4. Topic: Best places to shop in my town

   Method: Tell an anecdote.

_____

_____

_____

_____

5. Topic: How to resist advertising

   Method: Make opposing statements.

_____

_____

_____

_____

6. Topic: Tips for bargain shopping
   Method: Use a quotation.

_____

_____

_____

_____

Exercise 3.1b

On a separate page, select two of your opening statements and thesis statements from Exercise 3.1a and write a complete introductory paragraph for each.

Writing with a Purpose

The **body paragraphs** of your written piece contain the main points that you want to develop. Most essays have three or more body paragraphs. Each body paragraph should have a topic sentence based on the main headings in your outline. Just as the thesis statement provides a focus for the entire essay, a topic sentence provides a focus for its supporting paragraph. Each paragraph should be developed with supporting ideas and details.

THE TOPIC SENTENCE

To write a topic sentence, look at the word or phrase you have written in your outline and turn it into a sentence expressing the point you want to make. Here are some guidelines to help you write good topic sentences:

- A topic sentence summarizes the main point of the paragraph and tells the reader your point of view.
- A topic sentence should be the most general sentence in the paragraph.
- The topic sentence is usually the first sentence in the paragraph. However, you can place the topic sentence in the middle or at the end of the paragraph if it fits better there.
- The topic sentences from all the paragraphs in an essay should add up to a summary of the whole piece.

Exercise 3.2a

Below is an outline for the piece that was introduced in Lesson 1.

   I.   Introduction
  II.   Advertisments encourage impulse buying.
        A. We are bombarded with ads.
        B. Ads make us want things we can't afford.
 III.   Be a wise shopper.
        A. Decide what you really need.
        B. Look for the best prices.
  IV.   Make up a realistic budget.
        A. Identify your expenses.
        B. Know what you need to spend.
   V.   Stick to your budget.
        A. Develop a system.
        B. Save for "extras" and "treat yourself."
  VI.   Conclusion

Write a topic sentence for each of the main ideas in the above outline. The first one is done for you.

   1. II.   Advertisments encourage impulse buying

       Topic Sentence: Think of all the advertisements you see every day telling you to buy clothes, food, electronics equipment, cosmetics, liquor, and cigarettes, to name a few.

   2. III. Be a wise shopper

       Topic Sentence: _____

       _____

       _____

   3. IV.   Make up a realistic budget

       Topic Sentence: _____

       _____

       _____

   4. V.   Stick to your budget

       Topic Sentence: _____

       _____

       _____

SUPPORTING IDEAS AND DETAILS

Develop the body of the paragraph by giving examples, facts, and opinions or reasons that support your point. Examples usually are based on the writer's personal experience or observations. Facts consist of information that is true and can be proven. Sometimes a **source** or **authority** is provided for a fact such as a statistic. Opinions or reasons are yours or someone else's ideas. They should be logical and make sense to the reader, whether or not the reader agrees with them.

Include details that clarify and explain your point. Remember to avoid including unnecessary details. Too many details distract and confuse the reader. For instance, if you use a personal example of something that happened to you, it may not be necessary to tell when it happened or the exact circumstances.

Exercise 3.2b

Write a supporting paragraph for each topic sentence you wrote in Exercise 3.2a. Include an example, fact, and an opinion or reason. The first one is done for you.

1. Topic Sentence: Think of all the advertisements you see every day telling you to buy clothes, food, electronics equipment, cosmetics, liquor, and cigarettes, to name a few.

   Example: On the bus or subway, ads are placed directly in your line of vision. You begin to read them without even thinking.

   Fact: The remote control gives us one way to fight back when we are bombarded with ads on TV, but many people watch commercials anyway.

   Opinion or Reason: Obviously advertising works because companies spend millions and millions of dollars on it.

2. Topic Sentence: _____

   _____

   _____

   Example: _____

   _____

   _____

   Fact: _____

   _____

   _____

   Opinion or Reason: _____

   _____

   _____

3. Topic Sentence: _____

_____

_____

Example: _____

_____

_____

Fact: _____

_____

_____

Opinion or Reason: _____

_____

_____

4. Topic Sentence: _____

_____

_____

Example: _____

_____

_____

Fact: _____

_____

_____

Opinion or Reason: _____

_____

_____

The Conclusion

Once you have covered the main points in your piece, you don't want to leave your reader hanging. A conclusion is a way to "wrap up" your thesis and present it again to the reader in a repackaged form. For a piece of three or more paragraphs, you should write a conclusion that restates your thesis and summarizes your main ideas. If you write a short piece with a body of no more than two paragraphs, you may conclude with one or two sentences added to your last paragraph.

In a separate concluding paragraph, the topic sentence is usually a summary of your introductory paragraph or a restatement of the thesis. Don't bore the reader by using the exact wording used before. You can also add some additional information that is directly related to the main point of the piece. However, don't bring up new information or additional points that should have been covered in your body paragraphs.

Here is an example of a concluding paragraph:

> Advertisers want your money. It is up to you to resist giving it to them. Being aware of the effect ads have on you is the first step to overcoming impulse buying. Put yourself on a budget that you can live with. Challenge yourself every day to stick to it. The good feeling you get when buying something will be replaced with the good feeling of pride in yourself. You will be in control.

Exercise 3.3

On a separate page, use the above paragraph as a model and write a concluding paragraph to go with the supporting paragraphs you wrote in Exercise 3.2b.

Writing Assignments

Building Your Word Power

Write the Key Terms and Life Skill Words listed in the beginning of this chapter in your notebook. Break each word into syllables. Write an original sentence for at least five of the words. Then choose a few of the words and write synonyms for them.

Reading to Write

Go through the daily or Sunday newspaper. Read the ads and look for words, phrases, and sentences that are written to make the consumer have a strong desire for the item advertised. Write these words phrases and sentences in your notebook.

Chapter 4

Developing Rough Drafts

"What's wrong Marilyn?" asked Annie, the supervisor at the bakery where Marilyn worked. "You keep looking at the clock. Do you have to leave?"

"No, not really," said Marilyn. "I'm just anxious for the day to end. I'm worried about my little boy, Kevin."

"Why, is he sick?" Annie was concerned.

"I don't know what's wrong with him. But when I pick him up today, I'll find out if he's going to be kicked out of his day-care program." Marilyn looked sad and worried.

Kicked out of day care?" Annie tried not to laugh.

"It's not funny." Tears came into Marilyn's eyes. "Kevin seems angry all the time since his father and I separated. He has **temper tantrums,** and he cries a lot. Every day he gets into a fight and bites one of the other kids. Yesterday, the director said if it happens again, he can't come back."

"But isn't it normal for kids to bite each other?" asked Annie.

"The teacher said he should have developed past that stage by now. But I don't know anything about **stages of development.** I'm a mother, not a teacher," said Marilyn.

"Well, maybe you should do what my daughter did. She took a parenting class at the high school at night. She learned how to be a mother from an **expert.**

"The teacher was someone who specializes in **parenting education.** It's hard for parents to understand all the things that influence their children's lives. Especially young people like you. I'll call my daughter and you can talk to her about the program she took."

"Thanks Annie, " said Marilyn. "I feel much better now that I've talked to you."

Key Terms

- cause
- compare
- contrast
- effect
- rough draft
- space order
- time order

Life Skill Words

- expert
- immunization shots
- parenting education
- siblings
- stages of development
- temper tantrums

Time and Space

Each step in the writing process helps you clarify and organize your ideas. The first step in writing a complete piece is to develop a rough draft. A **rough draft** is your first attempt at putting your entire outline in paragraph form. At this stage you want to concentrate on getting your ideas down in complete sentences and in an order that makes sense. When you write a rough draft you should feel free to cross out words and sentences, make notes to yourself in the margins, and move sentences from one place to another. But don't get too caught up in revising. That will come later. Focus on the content and organization of your paragraphs without worrying about the finishing touches at this stage.

There are different methods you can use for presenting ideas and information in the paragraphs of your essay. One common method is time order. Time order means presenting information in order of when it occurred. **Time order** is commonly used in narration—telling a story or sequence of events. The following *signal words* can help your reader follow your meaning.

Signal Words for Time Order

after	later	the first thing
before	next	the next thing
finally	then	the last thing

You might also use words that refer to specific points in time, such as *yesterday, this evening, last month,* or *in May.* The following paragraph presents information in time order.

After Marilyn talked with Annie's daughter, she decided to take a parenting class. Later, she picked up Kevin and talked with the day-care worker. She told her that she was going to get some expert advice. Then she went to the high school to enroll in the parenting class. That same evening she talked with the instructor who gave her some good advice on how to handle Kevin. That night, when Marilyn tucked Kevin into bed, she talked to him about his father. She finally got Kevin to admit that he was angry about not being able to see his dad.

Exercise 4.1a

Place the sentences in a logical time order by putting the numbers 1–5 in the correct spaces. Find the topic sentence and make it #1. The first one has been done for you.

Paragraph 1

_____ After a week or so, if your baby is still crying hard when you leave, sleeping irregularly, or showing other symptoms of stress, talk to the daycare workers to find out why your child is not happy.

_____ For the next few days, you may need to take time during the day to stop in and spend some time with your child.

___1___ Parents can help their infants and toddlers adjust to being in a new child-care situation.

_____ If your child is not well adjusted and happy by the end of two or three weeks, maybe this is not the best day-care situation for your baby.

_____ At first, don't leave the child abruptly—try to stay until you feel the baby is beginning to relax.

Paragraph 2

_____ Over the weekend, I asked her to play school with her dolls and pretend that she was the teacher.

_____ Yesterday, when I picked up my four-year-old from her first day in a new preschool, she looked down at the ground and refused to talk.

_____ When something is wrong, young children may have trouble explaining how they feel.

_____ By listening to her play, I finally learned that she didn't like her new teacher and wanted her "old" teacher back.

_____ By Friday, she refused to go to school, but she would not tell me why.

Check your answers on page 121.

Another way to organize information is in terms of **space order.** Space order tells the relationship of one thing to another according to location. Space is often used in descriptive writing because it is a good way to give the reader a mental picture of a place. The following signal words can help your reader follow your meaning.

Signal Words for Space Order

above	beside	nearby	to the left
across	between	next to	to the right
across from	middle	on top of	
below	near	opposite	

The following sample paragraph uses space order.

The house was a mess and totally unsafe for children. When I opened the door, I noticed that just below the doorknob the paint was peeling. Down the hallway, I saw a loose rug that a child could easily trip on. On top of the tables there were small objects that a child could put in its mouth, and opposite the sofa was a window without safety bars.

Exercise 4.1b

Fill in the blanks with the appropriate space order word from the words listed below.

near   across   middle   above   between

To make a child's home safe, try to keep the child confined to a "childproof" area. (1) Place safety gates _____ doorways to keep the child out of the other rooms. (2) All small and breakable objects should be _____ the child's reach or out of sight. (3) The bars in the child's crib should be too narrow for the child's head to fit _____ them. (4) Create a play area with safe toys in the _____ of the room, away from any outlets on the walls. (5) Always stay _____ your child and sternly correct any unsafe behavior each time you observe it.

Check your answers on page 121.

Cause and Effect

One of the main reasons for writing is to explain something or answer a question. Most actions occur because of a cause, and most actions have an effect. A **cause** is what makes something happen. The thing that happens is the **effect.** When you discuss the causes and effects of an action, you make it understandable to your reader. The following signal words help connect causes and effects.

Signal Words for Cause and Effect

as a result	if	so
as a result of	then	so that
consequently	therefore	

The most common words used in cause and effect discussion are: *of course*, *because* or *because of*. The word *since* can also be used to mean because. Other common cause and effect words include *if, so that, as a result* or *as a result of, so* or *so that, then,* and *consequently.*

Cause and effect shows a relationship. This relationship can be discussed in whatever order suits your point of view. In some cases you may wish to state a cause in your topic sentence and support it with a list of effects. Other times it may be better to state an effect and support it with a list of causes.

Following are two examples.

Paragraph 1

Cause:	The government is cutting funding for child-care programs.
Effect:	Some parents will have to quit their jobs to stay home with their children.
Effect:	Child-care facilities will close and people will be unemployed.
Effect:	Some children will be left with people who are not qualified to care for them.

Paragraph 2

Effect:	Cutbacks in government programs will create hardships for parents.
Cause:	Parents will not be able to afford to pay for quality care.
Cause:	Parents will not have quality care centers available.
Cause:	Parents may have to quit work to stay home and care for their children.

Paragraph 1 discusses the effects of government cutbacks. Paragraph 2 discusses the causes of parents' hardships.

Exercise 4.2

For each topic sentence write supporting sentences that discuss causes or effects.

1. Topic Sentence/Cause: Smoking in the home is not good for children.

   Effect: _____

   _____

   Effect: _____

   _____

   Effect: _____

   _____

2. Topic Sentence/Cause: Children who don't get their **immunization shots** are at risk. (Note: immunization shots protect people from getting certain serious diseases.)

Effect: _____

_____

Effect: _____

_____

Effect: _____

_____

3. Topic Sentence/Effect: Community and family support helps single parents be good parents.

Cause: _____

_____

Cause: _____

_____

Cause: _____

_____

4. Topic Sentence/Effect: Parents are responsible when their children have poor eating habits.

Cause: _____

_____

Cause: _____

_____

Cause: _____

_____

Lesson 3
Compare and Contrast

When you want to discuss the similarities and differences among things, you can use the compare and contrast method of writing. When you **compare** two things, you point out the ways they are alike. When you **contrast** two things, you point out their differences. Words that are often used in compare/contrast paragraphs include the following:

Signal Words for Comparing and Contrasting

different	in comparison	same
differently	in contrast	similar
however	likewise	similarly

Here are two techniques for comparing and contrasting:

1. First describe the characteristics or details of one subject. Then show the similarities or differences of the other subject.
2. Alternate between similarities and differences for each characteristic or detail.

Here is an example of the first technique:

Children with older **siblings** (sisters and brothers) are usually ready to go to school. They want to be like the "older" kids, with books, new clothes, and friends to talk about. Their verbal skills are often more developed and they are often more mature. They are used to sharing toys and adult attention with other children.

On the other hand, an "only child" is often more attached to his or her home and parents. They haven't had role models to show them the positive side of leaving home for school. They are often less mature and may not talk as much as children with siblings. If they haven't been in day care, they have to be taught to share toys and attention.

Here is an example of the second technique:

Children with older siblings (sisters and brothers) are usually ready to go to school. On the other hand, an "only child" is often more attached to his or her home and parents. Children with siblings want to be like the "older" kids, with books, new clothes, and friends to talk about. In contrast, "only children" haven't had role models to show them the positive side of leaving home for school. Furthermore, children with siblings are often more mature. Their verbal skills may be more developed. They are used to sharing toys and adult attention with other children, while the only child has more to learn in this area.

Exercise 4.3a

For each sentence below, write a comparison or contrast sentence. The first one is done for you.

1. Years ago, parenting skills were passed from one generation to another within the family.

   Contrast with conditions today: Today family members often do not live in the same community.

2. Today fathers and mothers have more problems and less time to deal with their children.

   Contrast with conditions years ago: _____

   _____

   _____

3. Some parents use the television set as a "baby-sitter."

   Contrast with better child supervision:_____

   _____

   _____

4. Children are influenced by watching television from a very early age.

   Compare with adults: _____

   _____

   _____

5. Many people feel that parents have the main responsibility for teaching values to their children.

   Compare with school's responsibility: _____

   _____

   _____

   _____

6. Parents must be good role models because children imitate what they see adults do.

   Compare with babies' behavior: _____

   _____

   _____

Check your answers on page 121.

Exercise 4.3b

1. Write two paragraphs on the topic

   When it comes to nutrition, the media sends different messages to parents and children.

   In the first paragraph describe the messages that adults get. In the second paragraph describe the contrasting messages that children get.

2. Now rewrite your material comparing and contrasting the messages sent to adults and children within one paragraph.

Writing Assignments

Building Your Word Power

Write the Key Terms and Life Skill Words listed in the beginning of this chapter in your notebook. Break each word into syllables. Write an original sentence for at least five of the words. Then choose a few of the words and write synonyms for them.

Reading to Write

Read your local newspaper for a week. Clip or photocopy articles that discuss child-care, health, nutrition, education, and other programs that help young children in your community. In your notebook, write a summary of the information you found. Comment on whether or not the community does a good job of supporting children and parents.

- Use time or space organization to describe services available.
- Use cause and effect organization to show the results, problems, or successes.
- Use comparison or contrast to look at two different services or programs.

Chapter 5

Narrating

"Hey, Yoshio, wait up," Larissa called.

"Hi, Larissa! I haven't seen you at the clubs for weeks. What's going on?" Yoshio asked as he greeted his friend.

"Oh, I've been taking some night classes for my job. I don't have time for dancing right now. How's your sister Umeko?" Larissa asked.

"I'm not sure how she is, to tell you the truth. She seems **jittery** and **depressed**. I don't know—lately, she doesn't seem able to think clearly or make any decisions. I'm really worried about her," Yoshio said hesitantly.

"I know what you mean. I've noticed the same thing. You know, I think Umeko may have a problem with alcohol **dependence**," Larissa stated.

"Come on, Larissa. Umeko is a **social drinker** just like everyone else at the clubs. She has a few beers or a couple of glasses of wine. Are you saying that she's an **alcoholic**?" Yoshio asked in amazement.

"Well, she may not be an alcoholic, but she could be **abusing** alcohol. She seems to finish her drinks much faster than the rest of the gang. Before we went out on a double date a couple of months ago, she claimed that she needed a drink to get into the mood. And I've run into her a few times on Thayer Street during lunch hour. Yoshio, her breath smelled as if she had been drinking."

"You may be right, Larissa. What do you think we should do?" asked Yoshio in a concerned voice.

"Maybe we should try to talk with her about it before the problem becomes an **addiction**," Larissa answered.

Key Terms

- atmosphere
- character
- climax
- conflict
- dialogue
- incident
- interpret
- pace
- plot
- setting
- story map

Life Skill Words

- abusing
- addiction
- alcoholic
- dependence
- depressed
- jittery
- social drinker

What Makes a Good Story

Narration is a story told to make a point about something that happened. It's a good way to introduce or illustrate a subject. For example, you might want to persuade a group of young readers to wear helmets when bicycling. To begin you might narrate an **incident** (IHN-suh-duhnt), a situation or event, about how a helmet saved someone you know from serious injury. You can also use narration for its own sake—to provide a detailed, personal account of an experience and why it was important.

Regardless of how you use narrative writing, all good stories share certain important characteristics.

1. A good story has a **conflict**—a problem that a character must solve. In an external conflict, the character struggles against another person, nature, or society. In an internal conflict, the character struggles against himself or herself. For example, you might write about a person who decides not to do drugs in spite of pressure from his friends. In this case, the problem could be both external and internal. The character must take a stand against his friends, but he may also have to struggle against temptation and his own emotions.

2. A good story has a **plot**—a series of related events that grow out of the conflict and that make up the action of the story. Suspense mounts until you reach the **climax,** the tensest or most exciting part of the plot. This is where something happens to determine the outcome of the conflict.

3. A good story has a **setting.** It lets readers know when and where the action takes place. The setting also establishes an **atmosphere** (AT-muh-sfihr), a mood or feeling, for the conflict, such as unhappiness, danger, or excitement.

4. A good story has **characters**—believable people who reveal themselves through their words and actions. **Dialogue,** the words that characters exchange, can often provide important background information and reveal personality.

5. In addition to entertaining an audience, a good story should make a point. It should suggest some insight into human nature in general or the importance of the event in the writer's life.

Exercise 5.1a

For each of the plot situations given below, state the conflict and the main point you would make in a narrative. The first one is done for you.

1. *Setting:* a crowded public swimming pool on a hot summer day

   Character: Zeke, a 17-year-old boy who took a life-saving course during the school year

Plot: Zeke sees a young child fall into the deep end of the pool. The lifeguards are busy with other swimmers and no one else seems to notice.

Conflict: Zeke's conflict is internal. He wants to save the child, but he isn't sure he can remember everything he learned in the life-saving course. He's afraid he'll fail.

Main Point: By saving the child, Zeke overcomes his fear and increases his self-confidence.

2. *Setting:* high school cafeteria and ladies' room

   Characters: Elena and Rose are best friends. Rose is very thin and pale.

   Plot: The two girls have just finished lunch. Rose tells Elena that she has to go to the ladies' room and will see her later, but Elena follows her there and hears Rose vomiting.

   Conflict: _____

   _____

   _____

   Main Point: _____

   _____

   _____

3. Setting: a hospital waiting room

   Characters: Mr. and Mrs. Paranjpe and Dr. Johanson

   Plot: Dr. Johanson has just operated on Mrs. Paranjpe's mother. He discovered extensive cancer and has told the family that she doesn't have long to live. He has not told the patient, yet.

   Conflict: _____

   _____

   _____

   Main Point: _____

   _____

   _____

Check your answers on page 121.

DETERMINING THE MEANING OF AN EXPERIENCE

When you're caught up in the middle of an experience, it's tough to understand the impact of the event on your life. Therefore, when planning a narrative essay, you need to **interpret** (ihn-TER-preht), or explain the meaning of, the incident. This will help you to decide what makes the experience worth writing about. A checklist like the one below can help you to explore each aspect of the experience.

CHECKLIST FOR INTERPRETING EXPERIENCE

Experience: *Smoking my first cigarette in 7th grade*

This experience is important to me now because it

___✓___ helped me see something in a new way.

_____ changed the way I feel about myself.

I will always remember this experience because it

_____ strongly affected my attitudes.

___✓___ had important consequences in my life.

This experience is worth writing about because it

_____ will be familiar to many readers.

___✓___ gave me an insight that may help other people.

Interpretation: *That first cigarette made me realize that smoking would never make me look "cool" or get me into the "in" crowd.*

Exercise 5.1b

Think of a personal experience that fits one of the general categories below. Interpret the meaning the experience had for you by developing a checklist like the one above.

1. An experience that helped build your self-confidence
2. An experience that contributed to your understanding of a person
3. An experience that helped you to see your neighborhood or town in a new light

Selecting Details

An important part of developing a narrative essay is using details that will flesh out the event and bring it to life. First decide on the main point you want to make about the incident. Then list all of the details that will make readers feel as if they are at the scene with you. Jot down any factual information that will provide necessary background about the experience.

Before you start drafting, list vivid descriptive and sensory details that will spark your readers' imagination.

In the following example, the writer decided to narrate an embarrassing experience with head lice. Notice the different kinds of details she listed. Also notice the details she crossed out.

> *Thesis statement:* I learned the hard way not to lend my hairbrush to just anyone.
>
> Female headlouse lays as many as 300 eggs during its month-long life
>
> Eggs, called "nits," attach to hairs on person's head
>
> To eat, lice stab little holes in your scalp and suck blood
>
> ~~Friend, Lydia had fleas, but not as bad~~
>
> ~~Got fleas from pet cats~~
>
> Intense, painful itching from lice—can scratch until head bleeds but it will still itch
>
> Can see tiny, crawling insects with naked eye
>
> Need special medicine to get rid of the creatures—normal shampooing doesn't help
>
> Mother spent an hour a day removing nits with special fine-toothed comb (how the expression "nit picking" started!)
>
> ~~Scabies (another kind of bug) actually burrows under the skin~~
>
> Whole family has to use my shampoo
>
> Mother was the one to find them—she had noticed me with hands constantly in hair, scratching scalp
>
> She didn't need magnifying glass—simply parted the black strands and there they were, sucking away
>
> Terribly embarrassing—don't want anyone to know I have bugs
>
> Saying no to Tara and others about borrowing my brush will be much easier now

This is also a good time to weed out unnecessary details. Tracing every minute of an experience would be exhausting for you as the writer. It would also be boring for your readers. The idea is to highlight the important aspects of an incident. Remove anything that doesn't contribute to the main point you want to make. In the example above, the writer deleted details about other parasites like fleas and scabies. Although she originally considered comparing and contrasting these insects with head lice, she realized that this information would not show why and how she had learned not to lend her hairbrush to others.

Exercise 5.2

For each list of details, cross out any that should not be included in an essay based on the given thesis statement. On the lines below each group, explain why you eliminated these details. The first one is done for you.

1. *Thesis statement:* The day my grandmother blocked the door with chairs is the day the whole family realized that something was very wrong.

   Can't play cards anymore—said she wasn't interested but I knew she couldn't remember how to play

   Said she didn't recognize cousin Sally because Sally had dyed her hair, but Sally's hair has always been red

Scratched out women's faces in photo album that she doesn't like—Mom says it's because Grandma thinks Grandpa loves them, not her

Accused neighbor of stealing sweaters she misplaced

Grandma had managed for many years to run a home and raise a family, could follow detailed patterns to knit scarves and vests

At 74, she couldn't remember today's date or who is President

Grandma has Alzheimer's disease—like an eraser that slowly but surely rubs out a person's self

~~Accountants with Alzheimer's can't balance checkbook, football fans cannot follow the game~~

Reasons for deletion: <u>This detail has nothing to do with Grandma. They are other examples of what happens to people with Alzheimer's.</u>

2. *Thesis statement:* The physical effects of drug abuse can be very serious, but for me, the social effects were even worse.

Most drugs either stimulants or depressants—meant that I was either excitable, irritable, and aggressive or withdrawn and gloomy

Many young people begin because they are introduced to drugs by friends.

As drug use got heavier, cut off from normal life—friends and family annoyed or upset at unpredictable changes in my behavior, caused me to depend more heavily on drugs to avoid reality.

Some people start to take drugs out of curiosity or boredom.

Need lots of money to maintain habit—forced into crime to buy drugs.

Taking risks was fun at first, but stress and fear of being caught affected behavior, family life, school, and job.

Drug taking often gesture of defiance against authority

Reasons for deletion: _____

_____

_____

3. *Thesis statement:* Getting a tattoo was the worst decision I have ever made.

Thousands of beautiful designs to choose from.

Larue and Donnie had teased and pressured me, calling me "chicken" and "wuss."

Thought that getting it behind my knee would keep it a secret—forgot about gym shorts and bathing suit.

Tattoo studio in seedy part of town, filthy floor and tables (needles were probably dirty, too, but I didn't want to think about that)

Obviously awakened tattoo artist—he could barely see straight—drew the heart crooked and misspelled Suzette's name.

Lots of burning pain

Had to stand still for over an hour without bending knee

People have been tattooing and otherwise decorating their bodies since the first humans began living together in communities.

Two days later I was in the hospital with a high fever and a bad infection.

Tattoo permanent for me—can't afford laser treatment that would remove it.

On top of it all, Suzette broke up with me three weeks later—now I'll walk around with her name on the back of my leg forever.

Reasons for deletion: _____

_____

_____

Check your answers on page 121.

Lesson 3

Organizing the Narrative

Chronological order is well suited to narrative writing because it presents events in the order in which they occurred. In most cases you will want to tell your story from the first action to the last.

Chances are, your prewriting notes for your narrative are a series of random ideas. Now it's time to organize these notes. A formal outline identifying major topics and subtopics doesn't really fit this kind of writing. Instead, try a **story map** like this one.

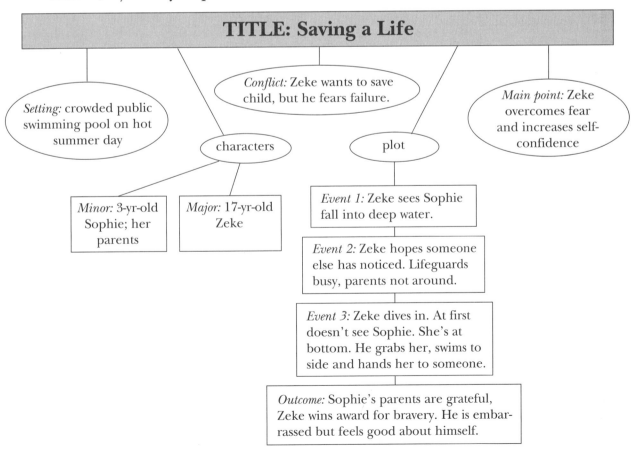

TITLE: Saving a Life

Setting: crowded public swimming pool on hot summer day

characters

Conflict: Zeke wants to save child, but he fears failure.

plot

Main point: Zeke overcomes fear and increases self-confidence

Minor: 3-yr-old Sophie; her parents

Major: 17-yr-old Zeke

Event 1: Zeke sees Sophie fall into deep water.

Event 2: Zeke hopes someone else has noticed. Lifeguards busy, parents not around.

Event 3: Zeke dives in. At first doesn't see Sophie. She's at bottom. He grabs her, swims to side and hands her to someone.

Outcome: Sophie's parents are grateful, Zeke wins award for bravery. He is embarrassed but feels good about himself.

Exercise 5.3

Choose one of the story situations in Exercise 5.1a, or a situation of your own and create a story map for it. Think of a title for the situation, then fill in the setting, characters, main point, and conflict. List the events in the order in which they happened. Be sure to include the outcome—how the problem is resolved and how the story ends. Use the story map above as a sample. Be sure to save your work.

Drafting the Narrative

Even though a narrative essay is less formal in structure than other types of essays, it should still have all the parts of any good piece of writing: an interesting introduction, an effective body, and a memorable conclusion.

DRAFTING THE INTRODUCTION

The first paragraph of your narrative essay should do several things:

- Arouse the curiosity of your readers, making them want to find out what happens.
- Give background including an introduction of the main character, the setting, and the conflict.
- Show the impact of the experience. Tell readers what the essay is about and give them a clue as to how you feel about your subject.

Notice how the writer of this introductory paragraph accomplishes all of these goals.

Actually saving a life is much different than the textbook explanation. This may seem obvious, but I never thought about it until a hot summer afternoon at Wheeler Pool. I was walking toward the diving board, thinking about wowing the girls with a powerful back flip, when a tiny, blond-haired child tumbled into the deep water right in front of me. Textbook diagrams and words flashed before my eyes. I couldn't remember a thing I had learned. In spite of getting a good grade in senior life-saving, I felt I couldn't save this child from drowning.

Exercise 5.4a

Using the story map you created in Exercise 5.3, write an introductory paragraph on a separate sheet of paper. Be sure to capture your readers' interest, establish the background of the story, and provide clues about how the experience affected you. Use the introductory paragraph above as a sample. Be sure to save your work.

DRAFTING THE BODY PARAGRAPHS

Now that you've grabbed your readers' attention, lead them through the experience as you tell how the event happened. Use your story map to trace the action. Aim for a good **pace,** which means keeping the narrative lively and interesting. The following suggestions will help you to draft your body paragraphs.

1. Tell the events of your story one step at a time in chronological order.

2. Use signal words for time order, such as *soon, then, finally, after a while,* and *at first* to keep your story on track from beginning to end.

3. Begin each major event in your narrative with a new paragraph. Careful paragraphing will help the pacing. It will also help your readers follow the action.

4. Use specific details to make your readers feel as if they are involved in the story.

5. Use dialogue to reveal character and to keep the story moving.

6. Make your audience eager to find out what will happen next by adding an element of suspense to your story. Don't reveal the climax and the solution to the character's problem until the end of the story.

Notice how the story of saving a life unfolds slowly in this body paragraph.

I expected an instant response to the emergency from the crowd, and I paused by the edge of the pool. The lifeguards were busy with other swimmers, though. The child's parents were nowhere to be seen, and even the swimmers close by didn't see a thing. It was up to me. Gathering my courage, I plunged into the water.

Exercise 5.4b

Using the story map you created in Exercise 5.3 and the introductory paragraph you wrote in Exercise 5.4a, draft at least one body paragraph for the narrative. Concentrate on telling the events in chronological order. Use the body paragraph above as a model. Be sure to save your work.

DRAFTING THE CONCLUSION

By the end of your narrative essay, the main character (you) should have solved the problem and learned something by doing so. Your audience should have the impression that you have been changed in some way by this experience. You may have developed a new outlook, achieved personal satisfaction, or discovered something about yourself.

Your ending should give your readers a sense of completion. Any one of the following ways to conclude a narrative essay will help you to leave a lasting impression.

1. Summarize the body of your essay or restate the main idea in a new way.

2. Refer to ideas in the introduction to bring your essay full circle.

3. Add an insight that shows a new or a deeper understanding of the experience.

4. Appeal to your readers' emotions.

Notice how the writer of the essay about saving a life uses some of these techniques to bring his story to a close.

I felt uncomfortable when Sophie's parents thanked me. Winning the town's award for bravery and getting my picture in the newspaper embarrassed me. I was no hero. I was simply a kid who had finally realized that I had learned a vital, real-life skill. Being a good student had paid off.

Exercise 5.4c

Using your story map from Exercise 5.3, the introductory paragraph from Exercise 5.4a, and the body paragraph(s) from Exercise 5.4b, draft a conclusion for your narrative essay. Use the concluding paragraph above as a model.

NARRATIVE ESSAY MODEL: A DIARY OR JOURNAL ENTRY

Writing in a diary or a journal is a way to keep track of what you're doing, thinking, and feeling. Although you may write in it every day, your entries should not simply list your physical activities. Instead, think of the diary or journal as a sourcebook— a place to collect and preserve ideas, problems, decisions, hopes, and dreams. You can record the most private things that only you will read, or you can share your writing with others as you see fit.

The following model shows you some of the characteristics of a diary or journal entry. In this example Umeko records her thoughts and feelings about what Larissa and Yoshio had to say about her drinking.

Date and time of entry

March 15, 19—
8:30 P.M.

Introducton: Sets scene, establishes people involved and the problem.

I don't think I've ever been so angry and hurt. Last night I met Larissa and Yoshio at Tropica, a new dance club downtown. After we got our drinks, my brother and my best friend attacked me. "You have an alcohol problem, Umeko," they announced like some sort of experts.

Body: Develops the action of the incident.

Oh, they were kind and gentle enough about it at first. Yoshio said everyone feels relaxed, and happy after a drink or two. I, however, end up slurring my words and becoming clumsy and uncoordinated—at least according to him. I defended myself and denied this kind of behavior, but he has noticed that hangovers have begun to make me late for work. Then Larissa chimed in and accused me of drinking at lunch time. She thinks I need alcohol in order to function. When she blamed my bad moods on drinking, I had enough. I walked out of the bar.

Conclusion: Discusses insight that grew out of conflict.

Now that I think about it, maybe Yoshio and Larissa are right after all. During or after a hard day at work, I really do want a drink. Sometimes that one drink becomes several, and I lose track. The next morning I feel terrible. I also feel guilty and promise myself that I won't binge like that again. I guess I shouldn't feel angry and hurt about what they said. Maybe I do have a problem with alcohol.

Writing Assignments

Reading to Write

Choose an article in the first section of a newspaper and read it carefully. Then use the facts about who, what, where, when, how, and why to turn the article into a narrative essay. Put yourself in the place of one of the people in the article, and tell the story as if it happened to you. Be sure that all of the events are in chronological order. Save your work in your Writer's Portfolio.

Writer's Portfolio Assignment

Choose one of the topics listed below, and write a narrative essay in the form of a diary or journal entry. Use Umeko's essay on the previous page as a model. Be sure to follow the prewriting, drafting, revising, and editing guidelines in Chapter 1 as well as the instruction in this chapter.

Topic choices:

My most embarrassing experience

My worst illness (or accident)

My first day on the job

Helping a close friend achieve a goal

Chapter 6

Describing

Luz had known for a while that Johnny was sick with **AIDS.** Still, it was quite a shock to pick up the phone and hear that he had died. She felt herself trembling and had to sit down. Then she realized that tears were silently rolling down her cheeks.

Johnny was the older brother of her old friend Emilia. He was a terrific guy, always in a good mood. He laughed often and told funny stories. He just had the knack of making people smile.

But Johnny could be serious too, and he really cared about other people. Luz remembered how he had comforted her when her grandmother was in the hospital, listening to her fears and giving her a hug. He was especially serious when it came to talking about AIDS.

"This is a bad disease, Luz," he said. "But you don't have to get it. Remember to be careful. You can't know whether someone is **HIV-positive** from the way he looks. So always, always make sure your man uses a **condom** during sex. Don't be embarrassed. It's vital to your health."

Luz had to smile when she thought about that conversation. It was so much like Johnny to be serious and funny at the same time. She was going to miss him very much.

Luz realized she wanted to let his family know how special she felt he was. Perhaps they would find some comfort in hearing how much he had meant to her as a friend.

Key Terms

- descriptive
- impartial
- objective
- space order
- statement of purpose
- subjective
- thesis

Life Skill Words

- AIDS
- condolence
- condom
- HIV-positive
- IV drugs
- needle exchange program
- safe sex
- sexually transmitted disease (STD)

Organizing Ideas

Lesson
1

Describing

Descriptive (dih-SKRIHP-tihv) writing creates a word picture of a person, a place, an object, or a scene. The image you create will depend on your point of view, the details you choose, and how you organize those details.

OBJECTIVE AND SUBJECTIVE POINTS OF VIEW

Objective (uhb-JEHK-tihv) description gives the plain facts. The writer's purpose is to be **impartial** (ihm-PAHR-shuhl). Suppose your nephew's pet dog is lost, and you want to write a notice to post at the supermarket. You must write a clear, accurate objective description so that anyone can recognize the dog. You take an objective point of view when you think about what your reader wants to know.

Subjective (suhb-JEHK-tihv) description not only gives information, it also creates a positive or negative feeling about what is described. Suppose your nephew wants to find a new home for his dog. You can use subjective description to give the positive impression that the dog will make a wonderful pet. You take a subjective point of view when you consider the impression you want to create.

CHOOSING DETAILS

This is Luz's **statement of purpose** or **thesis,** which names your topic and expresses your reason for writing. It may identify your audience and the outcome you intend, as well.

> Write a description of my friend Johnny in a letter of **condolence** to his family that will comfort them and express my feelings.

In this thesis Luz identifies her topic: a description of her friend. She also gives her reasons for writing: to comfort his family and express her feelings.

For any description, you must support your thesis. You must choose specific details about your subject that create an image to suit your purpose.

Descriptive details tell the reader about what you can see, hear, smell, taste, and feel. To find the right details, start by brainstorming about your topic. Ask yourself questions such as the following.

What does the person look like? act like? talk like?

What shape is the object? What size? color? speed?

Is this place noisy? quiet? dimly lit? hot? crowded? smoky?

CHOOSING AN ORGANIZATIONAL PATTERN

Your descriptive details must be organized into a pattern that is logical—one that makes sense to the reader.

To describe a scene, you can use **space order** development. Imagine yourself in one particular spot in the scene. Start to describe the scene from that spot, looking around from top to bottom, or from side to side, or in some other orderly way.

In an essay about a city street scene in summer, the writer of the following paragraph imagined herself above the scene and looking down. Can you see the space order development in the writer's paragraph?

> The breeze on the roof offered little relief on this hot day. Below me people sat on their window ledges and fanned themselves. The fire hydrant was open, and there was water in the street. Some children ran back and forth in the water, playing. They were squealing with happiness.

You can also use other organizational patterns in your descriptive writing:

Comparison and contrast

Cause and effect

Order of importance

Exercise 6.1a

Each item contains a thesis and a brainstormed list of details that support the thesis. For each item, do the following.

1. Choose one of these organizational patterns: space order development, comparison and contrast, cause and effect, or order of importance.

2. On a separate sheet, arrange the details in an outline that reflects the pattern you have chosen. The first one is done as an example.

Example: Thesis: Describe a day-care center playground so that parents see it as a safe place for their children to have fun.

List of Positive Details

climbing equipment at back—kids love it!

large yard—room to run around

fence strong, no holes

play turtles as you walk in—kids climb on them and ride

children all prekindergarten age

teachers smiling

teachers watching the kids

trees and flowers around the outside

Organizational Pattern ___Space order development___

Outline

  I. Walking into the yard
- A. Pleasant space—trees and flowers outside
- B. Play turtles to climb on and ride—as you walk in
- C. Large yard—room to run
- D. Climbing equipment at back
- E. Strong, secure fence

  II. Safe and friendly place
- A. Teachers to supervise play
- B. Teachers smiling and friendly

 III. A place to make friends
- A. Many kids of kindergarten age
- B. Children having a good time

1. Thesis: Describe a local social club in an essay to be read by the community board. High school students gather in the club after school because they do not have a community center nearby.

   List of Negative Details

   room dark and dingy—fire exit?

   cracked linoleum floor cluttered with litter

   sharp, burning smoke—hard to breathe

   people nodding out—on drugs?

   two kids drinking beer in the corner

   room smells of liquor

   video games—to attract kids?

   no athletic equipment or sports—not even a pool table!

   bartender—not interested in kids

   Organizational Pattern _____

   Outline (Use a separate sheet.)

2. Thesis: Describe to teenagers an experimental new health clinic that has just opened in the local high school. The clinic is designed to meet students' needs for important information on preventing AIDS and other health issues.

   List of Positive Details

   vase of fresh flowers in the waiting room—orange African daisies

   wall poster describing **safe sex**

   nurse polite, smiling—told me to take my time with the form

   examining room—new equipment, could weigh myself privately

   doctor talked about sex, even though I was too embarrassed to ask

   can bring your boyfriend or girlfriend along

   boxes of condoms—you can just take them

   not a long wait

bright, clean interior—yellow walls with green trim

toys for kids in waiting room

booklet on **IV drugs, needle exchange programs**

Patterns of Organization _____

Outline (Use a separate sheet.)

Check your answers on page 122.

Adding Details

Often, a writer has to add details to an outline to make the description more vivid. To do this, read each item in your outline, and ask yourself questions about its look, sound, smell, taste, and feel.

Suppose your outline says "Pleasant space—trees and flowers." Ask yourself, How many trees? How big are they? Does the light shine through the leaves? Do the leaves rustle in the breeze? What colors are the flowers? Are the blossoms large or small? Do they have a fragrance? How do the petals feel?

ADDING POSITIVE DETAILS

Look again at the paragraph about a city street in the summer on page 54. The writer decided to add more details. Notice how the added details, which are underlined, create a stronger, more lively impression of the scene.

> The breeze on the roof offered little relief on this <u>95-degree</u> day. <u>Heat seemed to rise in waves from the asphalt below.</u> Elderly ladies, their <u>hair covered in red and black and yellow cotton handkerchiefs</u>, sat on their window ledges, <u>towels around their necks</u>, fanning themselves with <u>scraps of paper</u>. Below, in the street, <u>a man with a wrench</u> had opened the fire hydrant, and <u>a loud torrent of water gushed</u> across the <u>black</u> surface of the street and against the <u>row of parked cars</u>. <u>Seven or eight</u> children ran back and forth through the <u>stream of icy water</u>, <u>squealing and shouting</u>. <u>They stomped their feet in the puddles that collected by the curb, splashing one another. They stood with their backs to the rush of water, laughing, then running off. They waved their tiny arms, wet and glistening, in the sunlight.</u>

Exercise 6.2a

Each item contains a brief outline for a descriptive passage. In the space provided, add descriptive details that create a more vivid picture. The first one is done as an example.

Example: Topic: My first apartment, which I share with my cousin

      I. Apartment faces a courtyard

        A. <u>Lamps on all day long—high electric bills</u>

     II. Room arrangement is unusual

        <u>A. Bathtub in the kitchen</u>

   III. Four stories with no elevator

        A. <u>Break a sweat climbing those stairs</u>

1. Topic: My mother's best friend

    I. Her looks

     _____

     _____

   II. Her voice

     _____

     _____

  III. How she acts with me

     _____

     _____

2. Topic: In a city park after dark

    I. Sun setting on an autumn evening

     _____

     _____

   II. Smells

     _____

     _____

  III. What the park sounds like

     _____

     _____

  IV. What you can see—and what you can't

     _____

     _____

ADDING NEGATIVE DETAILS

You need to be selective about the details you use. You can change the feeling of a description by changing the modifiers or by adding details that create a different picture.

The writer of the city street scene decided to rewrite the description as follows to give a negative impression. The added negative details are underlined.

> It was 95 degrees. Heat seemed to rise in waves from the <u>grimy asphalt</u>. Elderly ladies sat on their window ledges, <u>staring vacantly</u> ahead, fanning themselves with tattered scraps. Below, in the narrow street, someone had <u>wrenched open</u> the fire hydrant. A stream of water <u>droned monotonously</u> into the street, <u>swirling garbage and broken bottles against the row of abandoned cars</u>. Several children ran back and forth, back and forth through the water, <u>screeching wildly.</u> They scooped up the <u>filthy water</u> that collected in puddles by the curb, splashing one another. They stood still, <u>shivering</u>. They raised their <u>skinny</u> arms, waving <u>frantically</u> in the <u>glare</u> of the sun.

Exercise 6.2b

Look again at the outlines you filled in for Exercise 6.2a on page 57. Copy the printed outlines on a separate sheet, leaving out the details you added. Now add different details, to create a different impression. For example, if you used positive details in Exercise 6.2a, use negative details here. The first one is done as an example.

Example: Topic: My first apartment, which I share with my cousin

    I. Apartment faces a courtyard
       A. <u>No bright sunlight to wake me early on weekends</u>

    II. Room arrangement is unusual
       A. <u>Built our own wall unit to fit</u>

    III. Four stories with no elevator
       A. <u>Lost 2 pounds this month walking up</u>

1. Topic: My mother's best friend
   (Copy the outline from Exercise 6.2a onto a separate sheet.)

2. Topic: In a city park after dark
   (Copy the outline from Exercise 6.2a onto a separate sheet.)

Check your answers on page 122.

WRITER'S MODEL: LETTER OF SYMPATHY OR CONDOLENCE

You can write a letter of sympathy, or condolence, to express your feelings and offer comfort when someone you know is very ill or has died. Even if you decide to send a sympathy greeting card, you can add a handwritten note that your reader will appreciate.

As an informal personal letter, a letter of sympathy may leave out an inside address. Use a salutation that suits your relationship. The body of the letter usually starts with an expression of how sorry you feel about the death or illness. Then, if you like, you might write a few lines about the person—perhaps tell a positive memory you have. Finally, end with a sympathetic comment. If you can make a specific offer of help, do so. The closing is usually personal. "Love" is a good choice in a time of crisis.

Here is the letter that Luz wrote to Johnny's sister Emilia and his mother, Alicia, whom she always called "Auntie." The return address and inside address is required for a formal letter, but may be left off an informal note like this one.

Return address (optional in informal letter) Date	413 Irving Avenue, Apt. 4b Miami, FL 33187 June 7, 19—
Inside address (optional in informal letter)	Emilia and Alicia Martinez 2180 Holland Avenue, Apt 1c Miami, FL 33189
Informal salutation	Dear Emilia and Auntie Alicia,
Expression of sorrow	I was very, very sorry to hear about Johnny. I knew he was sick, but it still came as a shock to hear that we lost him.
Positive description	Johnny was always the wonderful big brother with a warm smile. He could cheer you up and make you feel good, no matter what happened. I remember how he listened to me and hugged me when my grandmother was in the hospital. I'll miss him very much, and I know that he had many other friends who loved him and will miss him too.
Offer of help	I will be back home at my mother's house next month. I'll call and come over to see you both.
	Love,
	Luz

SKILLS REVIEW: COMPARISON AND CONTRAST

You can use comparison and contrast to describe the similarities and the differences between two people, places, objects, or scenes.

In block format, you describe one subject and then the other. In alternating format, you go back and forth between the two subjects, comparing and contrasting them on different points. Which format is used in the essay that follows?

MY TWO BOSSES

My experience with employers leads me to the surprising conclusion that the nicest person is not necessarily the best boss.

My first boss, Rosemary, was a cold person. She never chatted with me and never, ever mentioned her personal life. Laura, who took over when Rosemary was promoted, was much more casual and friendly. We went out for lunch together and really got to know each other.

Rosemary was a real perfectionist. If you were late, she got annoyed. She just had to tell you to get in on time. If you typed a letter with an error, she made you do it over until there were absolutely no mistakes. Laura, on the other hand, never seemed to notice what time people arrived in the morning. And she never gave me typing to correct. Everything I did seemed to be just fine.

Of course, I preferred working for Laura. I really thought she was a great boss—until I changed jobs. That's when I saw that I had learned a lot more from Rosemary than from Laura.

Because Rosemary insisted on promptness, I had learned to arrive at work on time. At my new job, employees were fined when they were late. And because of Rosemary, I had learned to concentrate hard on doing work well the first time. When my new employer saw how good my work was, he promoted me very quickly.

Laura and I are still friends. But, considering everything, I have to say that Rosemary was the better boss.

Building Word Power

Add to your word notebook the Key Terms and Life Skill Words from this chapter. Break each word into syllables. Write an original sentence for at least five of the words. Then choose a few of the words and write synonyms for them.

Reading to Write

Read through magazines and newspapers for descriptive writing. Try articles that describe clothing fashions, interior decoration, and new car models, for example. You may also find descriptive passages about neighborhoods or holiday scenes. Clip or photocopy the passage, and add it to your portfolio. Write whether the description is objective or subjective. For subjective description, write if the feeling is positive or negative. Underline at least one detail in each passage that illustrates your conclusions.

Writer's Portfolio Assignment

Choose two topics from those listed below or use two of your own. For each topic, write a brief descriptive paragraph that is either objective or subjective. Use space order development for one paragraph and a different pattern of organization (comparison and contrast, cause and effect, order of importance) for the other paragraph. Keep the paragraphs in your portfolio.

The street I live on

The car I want to own

A music video I hate

The scene of a car accident

A concert I attended

A special meal I prepared

Chapter 7

Informing

"Thirty-three kids in a second-grade class! How can any learning go on in there?" David found himself speaking up at the **Parent-Teachers Association (PTA)** meeting at his daughter Janet's school.

"What can we do about this?" he asked.

The PTA president looked at the assembled parents. "We need strong leadership," she said. "We need **school board** members who will fight in the **state legislature** (LEHJ-uh-slay-chuhr) for more money for our schools. We need **representatives** (rehp-rih-ZEHNT-uh-tihvz) and **senators** who will fight for our kids in **Congress.**"

Parents all around him were nodding eagerly. David felt he just had to do something.

"We need a plan of action," David said, standing up. "We need to get together and tell the people in **government** what is going on. Many of us are **citizens,** and most of us are **taxpayers.** We have a right to be heard!"

Key Terms

- bullet
- informative
- irrelevant
- letterhead
- logical order
- memorandum (memo)
- newsletter
- opinion
- process order
- relevant
- report
- statistics

Life Skill Words

- campaign
- citizen
- Congress
- government
- Parent-Teachers Association (PTA)
- representatives
- school board
- senator
- state legislature
- taxpayer

Keeping Your Audience and Purpose in Focus

One common purpose of writing is to explain, illustrate, or instruct. As you learned in Chapter 1, this is called **informative** writing. The main uses of informative writing are:

1. To give factual information, answering the following questions about a situation or event: who? what? where? when? and how?

2. To give step-by-step directions, instructions, or explanations.

3. To make an idea or situation easier to understand by defining, illustrating, or explaining it.

Before you write, make sure you have a clear idea of your audience and your purpose. Choose the facts that support your purpose.

INCLUDE THE IMPORTANT FACTS

In any form of writing, try to include only information that is **relevant**, or related to your purpose. **Irrelevant** information may be interesting, but it does not fit the purpose of the piece you are writing. These details may confuse your reader. Follow these basic guidelines.

- Give all the important facts—numerical and otherwise.
- Omit facts that are not important to your purpose.
- Do not give your **opinion** (uh-PIHN-yuhn) about the facts.

David is writing a **report** for the school board on overcrowding in the classroom. David collected the important **statistics** (stuh-TIHS-tihks), or numerical facts. For each class, he listed the number of students allowed by law and then the actual number of students registered.

David gave other facts too. He described how children worked on the floor because they had no desks and shared textbooks because there were not enough classroom materials.

David did not include irrelevant information, such as how inexperienced some teachers were. Also, he was careful not to give his opinions about the overcrowding. He let the facts "speak for themselves."

In the **memorandum (memo)** that follows, the writer has included irrelevant facts, which are underlined once, and opinions, which are underlined twice. Has the writer left out any important information?

TO: Department Managers
FROM: Office Manager, Ext. 555
DATE: December 10, 199-
SUBJECT: Coffee Breaks

<u>I am very sorry to have to make these changes.</u>

<u><u>In the past we have had a very easygoing coffee break policy.</u> When I started here fifteen years ago, you could go for coffee whenever you wanted.</u> <u><u>But workers today seem to have no self-control.</u></u> <u>Anyway, the noise level is getting too great.</u>

Starting Monday, only two staff members from every department will be allowed on coffee break at the same time. Each employee should take no more than ten minutes.

Managers in each department are responsible for creating a coffee break schedule. Please give me a copy of your schedule on Monday afternoon. <u>Although I will be out of the office, just leave the schedule on my desk.</u>

If you have any questions, please call me.

Exercise 7.1a

In the memo that follows, draw a single line under facts that are irrelevant to the purpose of the memo. Draw two lines under statements that are opinions. Use the memo "TO: Department Managers" on this page as an example.

TO: Office Staff
FROM: Benefits Supervisor
DATE: April 17, 199-
SUBJECT: Approval for Dental Procedures

People keep asking me about this. So I decided to write a memo, even though all this information is in the Employee Handbook.

To file a claim for any kind of dental work except a routine exam, X rays, and cleaning, you must first apply for approval for the procedure. I find this very frustrating, but that's life.

The approval forms are on a clearly marked shelf in my office. Take a form and have your dentist fill it out and send it to the insurer. The address is on the form. When the dentist gets the approval, you can go ahead with the procedure.

I have done this myself, and it does actually work. Good luck!

Check your answers on page 123.

CHOOSE THE APPROPRIATE FORMAT

In addition to reports, other formats are used in personal and business writing to inform or explain:

- **Memo.** Use a memo to write to another person in your own organization, company, school, or other group. Write a memo on plain white paper or special memo stationery.

- **Business letter.** Use a business letter if you are an employee writing to someone outside your company. Write a business letter on company **letterhead** stationery.

- **Personal business letter.** Use a personal business letter if you are writing as an individual to a company, government agency, or some other organization. Write a personal business letter on plain white paper.

Exercise 7.1b

Each item states the purpose and the audience intended for a piece of informative writing. In the spaces provided, write the correct format to use: memo, business letter, or personal business letter. An example is done for you.

Example: *Purpose:*   To accept a job offer
          Audience: Future employer
          Format: <u>Personal business letter</u>

1. *Purpose:*   To explain a child's absence from school
   Audience: Child's teacher

   Format: _____

2. *Purpose:*   To give instructions on mailing procedures
   Audience: New employees at your company

   Format: _____

3. *Purpose:*   To invite a guest speaker to talk at your school's career night
   Audience: Executive from a major accounting firm

   Format: _____

4. *Purpose:*   To inquire about replacement parts for your company's equipment
   Audience: Equipment manufacturer

   Format: _____

5. *Purpose:*   To give directions to the new convention center
   Audience: Your company's salespeople

   Format: _____

Check your answers on page 123.

SKILL REVIEW: LISTS USING NUMBERS AND BULLETS

If a sentence lists five or more items, rewrite the sentence as a list with numbers or **bullets**—large black dots—to make reading easier. If the items in your list are long or if they contain verbs, you should start each item with a capital letter and end it with a period.

Use numbers in a list to highlight the *order* of steps or instructions. In the following instructions, each numbered step starts with a verb. When you separate a numbered item into parts, use a letter to start each part. Notice that some instructions also give the results you can expect or the reasons for the step.

To care for a child's minor cut or scrape:

1. Calm the child.
2. Control and stop the bleeding.
    a. Place a clean, sterile gauze pad or cloth over the cut or scrape.
    b. Press firmly and steadily until the bleeding stops, usually five to ten minutes.
3. Clean the cut or scrape to prevent infection.
    a. Scrub very gently with warm water and soap to remove all foreign matter. This may sting slightly.
    b. Rinse the area under warm running water for several minutes.
    c. Pat the area dry with a clean gauze pad or cloth.
4. Dress the cut or scrape.
    a. Use an adhesive strip (or a gauze pad and tape) large enough to comfortably cover the area.
    b. Apply a small amount of antiseptic ointment to the bandage to prevent sticking if the scrape is large.

Bullets do not emphasize sequential order as much as numbers do. However, they are good for separating items in a list, and they do make writing easier to read. Compare the following two passages. Even though the wording is the same, the passage with the bullet list is easier to read.

In order to get your child into kindergarten, you must take your child to a doctor or clinic for vaccinations, make sure to have the vaccination card filled out, get a utility bill or other proof of address, bring your child and the two proofs to the school office by September 1, and fill out a registration card.

In order to get your child into kindergarten, you must:

*   Take your child to a doctor or clinic for vaccinations.
*   Make sure to have the vaccination card filled out.
*   Get a utility bill or other proof of address.
*   Bring your child and the two proofs to the school office by September 1.
*   Fill out a registration card.

A memo or letter must be organized clearly and efficiently. The reader needs to get the important information quickly and easily. For a successful memo or letter, use the following organization.

- Opening—statement of purpose. Tell the reader the reason you are writing the memo or letter. Your statement of purpose can be a request for action.
- Body—support paragraphs. Give the reader the facts that support your purpose.
- Conclusion—a brief, appropriate ending. The conclusion can contain a request, recommendation, or question.

MEMO FORMAT

David wrote the following memo to the PTA president. The opening (statement of purpose), the body (support paragraphs), and the conclusion are labeled.

TO:	Vernetta Bell
FROM:	David Brodsky
DATE:	October 10, 199-
SUBJECT:	Report on Overcrowding

Opening   Attached is a copy of my report on overcrowding in the classes at our school. Please write any comments you have on a separate sheet.

Body   To write this report, I looked at the registration for each class. I also studied the school board rules to find out what the class sizes are supposed to be. Out of 21 classes, 17 have more students than the legal limit. Moreover, 12 of these classes have four or more students over the limit.

In the report, I also mention some of the effects of this overcrowding, such as children having to work on the floor or share textbooks.

Conclusion   Please get your comments to me by October 12 so that I can make the changes and distribute the report by October 14.

Exercise 7.1c

Each of the following items gives a statement of purpose and a list of facts and opinions. Mark the facts *F* and the opinions *O*. Include the facts in a memo that supports the statement of purpose. You can rewrite the facts in your own words. Write each memo on a separate sheet. Remember to use a memo heading and to include an opening, supporting body paragraphs, and a conclusion. Refer to David's memo "SUBJECT: Report on Overcrowding" on this page as an example.

1. Statement of purpose: To explain to teenagers working part-time at your company, how to dress at work

_____ a. Modern fashions are too sexy for work.

_____ b. No sandals or backless dresses are allowed in the summer.

_____ c. Men do not have to wear their jackets at their desks.

_____ d. Women may wear slacks, skirts, or dresses.

_____ e. Leave your fancy dress clothes at home.

_____ f. Ties are required for men.

_____ g. It doesn't matter if you wear makeup or not.

_____ h. It gets cold, so women might like to wear jackets or sweaters.

2. Statement of purpose: To request a leave of absence to care for a newly adopted baby

_____ a. We've waited years to be able to adopt a baby.

_____ b. We're both very happy, but nervous too.

_____ c. The company policy for new parents is a six-month leave without pay.

_____ d. My last day of work will be February 4.

_____ e. The policy states that you can return to the same job after six months.

_____ f. I will return to work on August 4.

Check your answers on page 123.

BUSINESS LETTER FORMAT

When you write a letter, remember that the reader will be a person outside your company or organization. Therefore, you may have to supply more identifying details to make the information clear. Notice the details about Carmen Hernandez in the following letter.

Filbert Motors Company
78541 Flatbush Avenue
Brooklyn, New York 11234

April 2, 199-

Ms. Louise Jones
White Mountain Travel Service
4655 West 42nd Street
New York, NY 10016

Dear Ms. Jones,

Please make reservations for Carmen Hernandez, our sales manager, at the Hotel San Antonio for Sunday, May 12, and Monday, May 13.

Opening

Ms. Hernandez will be arriving after 6 p.m. on the 12th. She would like a nonsmoking room with a double bed, near the courtyard, if possible.

Body

Please charge the room to the Filbert Motors Company account, and send a confirmation to Ms. Hernandez at the Sales Department, 4th floor.

If you have any questions, please call me at 555-4662. Thank you for your prompt attention.

Conclusion

Sincerely,

Karen Takao

Karen Takao
Personnel Department

Notice that the letter begins with an opening that states the purpose. Two body paragraphs provide details that support the purpose. The reader will know what services to provide and how to charge their cost. The letter ends with a conclusion. When you write business or personal business letters, follow this format. For personal business letters, include your address above the date (unless you use personal letterhead stationery).

Exercise 7.1d

Each item gives a statement of purpose and a list of facts and opinions. Mark the facts *F* and the opinions *O*. Include the facts in a business letter or a personal business letter that supports the statement of purpose. You can rewrite the facts in your own words. Write each letter on a separate sheet. Find appropriate addresses for these letters, or make them up. Remember to use a proper format and an opening, body, and conclusion for each letter. Refer to Karen Takao's letter to White Mountain Travel Service on page 69 as an example.

1. *Statement of purpose:* To request a social security card application for my child

   _____ a. My child is two years old.

   _____ b. My child's name is Ramon.

   _____ c. My child was born on March 20, 199-.

   _____ d. Please send a form for me to fill in.

   _____ e. Where do I send the completed form?

   _____ f. Is it true that I have to send his birth certificate?

   _____ g. It's annoying to have to spend so much time on this.

   _____ h. It's stupid that little kids need these cards.

2. *Statement of purpose:* To inform the staff of a local community center about part-time jobs available at your video production studio

   _____ a. We have jobs for people who are sixteen or older.

   _____ b. Kids will love working here.

   _____ c. The hours are 3:30 to 6:30.

   _____ d. They can't work more than three days a week.

   _____ e. We are paying $5.50 an hour.

   _____ f. Our pay is great, since other studios pay only $4 an hour.

   _____ g. Duties involve cleaning up before shoots and running errands.

   _____ h. People under 18 need working papers.

   _____ i. They should fill out and send in the enclosed application.

Check your answers on page 123.

Writing Directions

Instructions and directions are kinds of informative writing. How to install a CD player, how to cook fried chicken, how to get to your new job—all these are examples of informative writing.

To give instructions or directions, use **process order**, a kind of time order that breaks a task into steps. First, divide the activity into steps that go in sequence, one after another. Then write about each step in order.

To write clear instructions or directions, ask yourself these questions.

1. What equipment is needed?
2. What special conditions must there be?
3. What step is done first? second? next? and so on?
4. Do any big steps consist of smaller steps that must be done in order?
5. What should be the result after each step is completed?
6. What should be the final result after the final step?

An example of an essay written in process order follows. David and other parents met to discuss the overcrowding in the classes. In this essay David described their plan to start a letter writing **campaign** (kam-PAYN) in a memo to the PTA president. Notice that the memo explains the plan through process order development—step by step.

TO: Vernetta Bell
FROM: David Brodsky
DATE: October 20, 199-
SUBJECT: Letter-writing Campaign

The PTA committee on overcrowding met on October 19. We want more parents to know about the problem, and we want the school board to know that the PTA is concerned about it.

We decided to start a letter-writing campaign. We'll ask parents to write letters to the school board explaining the overcrowding and the problems it creates.

Sylvia Nieves will write a model letter that parents can copy. She will list the names and addresses of the school board members.

Nancy Wilson has volunteered to type the letter after work. Using PTA funds, we will make 100 copies of the letter. Mark Chu has offered to do the photocopying.

Meanwhile, Christina and Gus Costas will create two posters about the campaign and display the posters at the school entrances.

Finally, on the morning of October 28, several PTA members will give out the letters to parents. We will stand at the two school entrances and explain to parents why they should send letters to the school board.

If you have any suggestions to make about this campaign, please call me at home tonight or tomorrow. I can be reached at 555-0000

Notice that the memo includes an opening paragraph and a concluding paragraph. The body paragraphs are organized in process order. Each paragraph describes one step, and these steps are presented in time order. The information about the posters (paragraph 5) could have come earlier, since posters could have been hung before the model letter was drafted. The posters had to be hung before the model letters were given to parents, however, so this step was placed just before the final event. Often the information you have to give your reader does not follow a step-by-step process. In these situations use **logical order** to organize your thoughts. Begin by stating the problem or the idea. Then provide the facts that the reader needs in order to help you.

Also, whether you are writing for a business or personal reason, remember to include your contact information. Your reader needs this information to get in touch with you. Include your return address and telephone number if your reader needs to contact you.

Exercise 7.2

Each item gives a statement of purpose and a list of statements. Some statements are *relevant:* they fit the purpose because they instruct, explain, or direct. Some statements give *irrelevant* information or opinions. Mark each relevant statement *R* and each irrelevant statement *I*. Then arrange the relevant information in sequential order. On separate sheets write a brief letter that supports each statement of purpose. Use the letter from Filbert Motors on page 69 as a model of letter format. Refer to David's memo "SUBJECT: Letter-writing Campaign" on page 71 as an example of logical and process order writing.

1. *Statement of purpose:* Write a letter to the electrician explaining the problem with your lights.

   _____ a. We changed all the fuses after the lights blew out.

   _____ b. Lights blew out in living room and kitchen.

   _____ c. My son was very angry because he couldn't watch the ball game.

   _____ d. The fuse box is in the kitchen above the refrigerator.

   _____ e. The lights stayed off even after we changed the fuses.

_____ f. The superintendent said the main circuit breaker in the basement was working.

_____ g. Leave the key with the superintendent when you are done.

_____ h. Get the key from the superintendent if we are not home.

2. *Statement of purpose:* Write a letter to a friend who will visit soon. Explain how to get to your office from your home. (Assume she knows how to get to your home.)

_____ a. It takes less time if you take two buses, but there is also a way to get there with just one bus.

_____ b. Get the second bus at the corner of Ninth Avenue and 23rd Street, going south. The stop for the second bus is in front of a newspaper stand.

_____ c. First, take the bus three blocks from my house.

_____ d. Go out of my building and turn left and walk one block. At Fourth Avenue walk south three blocks to 23rd Street.

_____ e. Take the bus on 23rd Street going west and get off at Ninth Avenue. You'll pass the Bunny-Hop Inn on the way.

_____ f. Get off the second bus at 16th Street, cross Ninth Avenue, and there's my office.

_____ g. The office address is 70-59 Ninth Avenue, and the phone number is 555-7863.

3. *Statement of purpose:* Write a letter to an auto mechanic explaining the problem with your car.

_____ a. The car is old, so I expect some problems.

_____ b. Another mechanic already replaced the starter.

_____ c. Sometimes when I turn on the ignition, the car doesn't start at all. There is no sound or anything.

_____ d. The problem of not starting seems to happen in humid weather.

_____ e. You said on the phone that it could be the battery, the ground wires, or the starter.

_____ f. The battery is new; I bought it three months ago.

_____ g. I am getting very angry about this problem.

_____ h. Another problem is that the car stalls in cold weather.

Answers will vary. Check your answers on page 123.

WRITER'S MODEL: NEWSLETTER

One format used to convey information to large numbers of people is the **newsletter.** A newsletter is a small publication, usually just two to four pages. An organization such as a church may publish a newsletter to tell its members news and other information of interest. Unlike a newspaper or magazine, a newsletter usually has no advertising.

Articles in a newsletter follow news story format.

- The headline usually contains a verb.
- The first paragraph, called the lead, tells the "five W's" of the story—who, what, where, when, and why.
- The subsequent paragraphs give more detail and explanation.
- The article may contain direct quotations from people.
- The writer never gives his or her own opinions, recommendations, or conclusions.

Here is an article that appeared in the newsletter published by David's PTA.

PTA MEETS WITH BOARD MEMBER TO DISCUSS CLASS SIZE

On November 16, 199-, the president and other members of the Parent-Teachers Association met with Hector Otero of the Community School Board to express their concern about overcrowding of the classes at our school.

The PTA presented Mr. Otero with a report on the subject prepared by David Brodsky, a parent at the school. The report showed that 17 of 21 classes exceeded the legal limit in number of students, and that 12 of those classes had at least four students more than the limit.

Referring to the many letters received from parents at our school, Mr. Otero said that the board was aware of the overcrowding.

"We are all very concerned about this situation," he said, "The school population increased by 20 percent in the last two years. There aren't enough classrooms in the existing school buildings for all the children. Also, it's very hard to find competent teachers willing to work under these conditions."

Mr. Otero said he would discuss the matter with the other school board members and come up with some recommendations. He agreed to meet with the PTA members again on December 15, at 8 p.m. in the district office.

Writing Assignments

Building Your Word Power

Add to your word notebook the Key Terms and Life Skill Words from this chapter. Break each word into syllables. Write an original sentence for at least five of the words. Then choose a few of the words and write synonyms for them.

Reading to Write

Read through magazines and newspapers for informative writing. Look for news articles, how-to articles, and travel articles. Clip or photocopy at least two passages, and add them to your portfolio. Write whether each passage (1) gives factual information, (2) gives directions or instructions, or (3) clarifies a subject. Underline at least one sentence in each passage that supports your conclusions.

Writer's Portfolio Assignment

Choose two topics from those listed below or use two of your own. For each topic, write a brief informative paragraph that (1) gives factual information, (2) gives directions or instructions, or (3) clarifies a subject. Keep the paragraphs in your portfolio.

How to apply eye makeup

How to change a car tire

Who is in charge of what on my job

Getting to the movies from my sister's place

Toys that children like—and why

My future plans

Persuading

Kendra Greene looked straight at the television camera. Behind her, friends and neighbors were holding placards and shouting "Parks, yes! Pollution, no!"

"We have put up with enough!" Kendra said. "The **mayor** and **City Council** (KOWN-suhl) have treated our neighborhood like a dumping ground for projects that other communities don't want. Well, this **sewage** (SOO-ihj) **treatment plant** is the last straw. We'll fight it, and we'll win!"

Kendra held her own placard up to the camera for a moment. Then she walked back to her spot in the **picket line** that extended—one hundred people strong—along the bank of the river.

Key Terms

- authority
- editorial
- evidence
- letter of request
- letter to the editor

- op-ed page
- opinion
- persuasive
- summary

Life Skill Words

- City Council
- Environmental Protection Department
- First Amendment
- mayor
- picket line

- political action committee (PAC)
- sewage treatment plant
- state insurance commission

Organizing to Persuade

Persuasive writing is meant to convince you to hold a certain **opinion** or belief. We use persuasive writing when we want the audience to agree with our beliefs or to take the actions we suggest.

An **editorial** (ehd-uh-TOHR-ee-uhl) in a newspaper or magazine is an example of persuasive writing. The editors express their opinion and often urge citizens or public officials to act. Persuasive articles and columns also appear on the **op-ed page**—the page opposite the editorials—in a newspaper. Another example of persuasive writing is the text of a sermon. Sermons usually press listeners to act in a certain way—to pray, or to do good works, for example.

We also use persuasive writing in business and personal letters. A letter that recommends a friend for a job or asks for a refund will use persuasive writing.

Persuasive writing contains three parts.

1. Thesis. The thesis states your opinion or request. Put the thesis in the very first paragraph.

2. Body—support. The body contains **evidence** (EHV-uh-duhns), or proof, meant to convince the audience.

3. Conclusion—**summary.** The conclusion gives a summary, or brief review, of the points you have made and restates your opinion. Sometimes a request is given here.

Exercise 8.1a

For each of the following topics, write two opinions—one that is pro (in favor) and one that is con (against). The opinions may not be your own. An example is done for you.

Example: *Topic:* Capital punishment

    Pro: <u>Capital punishment is a just and fitting penalty for many horrible crimes.</u>

    Con: <u>Capital punishment is a barbaric penalty that expresses revenge, not justice.</u>

1. *Topic:* Mercy killing of dying people

    Pro: _____

    Con: _____

2. *Topic:* Segregating schools by race

Pro: _____

Con: _____

3. *Topic:* Free medical care for the poor

Pro: _____

Con: _____

4. *Topic:* Using animals for laboratory research

Pro: _____

Con: _____

Check your answers on page 123.

PUT YOUR OPINION FIRST

In persuasive writing, it is very important to state your opinion up front. Look at the following letter written to a rock music magazine. Can you tell what the writer's opinion is? What does the writer want?

Dear Editor,

Some people think music videos should be rated, like movies. The ratings would warn parents about the videos. Then parents could forbid their kids to watch the videos. Other people don't like this idea. They think that ratings would be against the **First Amendment**, which guarantees freedom of expression. They also think that the ratings would not stop kids from watching.

Sincerely,

Ralph McInnes

The writer has not stated his opinion. The letter gives us some information, but it does not persuade us to have a certain belief or to perform an action.

Now read Kendra Greene's **letter to the editor** of the local newspaper. A letter to the editor usually expresses an opinion about an article or a current issue. Sometimes it simply gives information. Kendra belongs to a political (puh-LIHT-ih-kuhl) **action committee**, or *PAC*, called CASP. In the letter that follows, Kendra's opinion is underlined once. Her request for action is underlined twice.

Dear Editor,

<u>The **Environmental Protection Department**'s plan to build a new sewage treatment plant in the Tidemark neighborhood is unfair.</u>

Just three years ago, the city's water purification plant was built here. In addition, Tidemark has two city dumps while some neighborhoods have none.

We are responsible citizens. We realize that these services must be located somewhere. However, our community should not have to shoulder more than its fair share.

<u><u>We, the members of CASP (Citizens Against Sewage Pollution), call for the EPD to abandon its current plan and find a new location for the plant.</u></u> Concerned citizens can call CASP at 555-1200, for information on how to help.

Sincerely,
Kendra Greene

Exercise 8.1b

Read each of the following letters. Write an opinion at the beginning and a request for action at the end. An example is done for you.

Example: Dear Editor,

<u>Automobile insurance companies discriminate unjustly against young adults.</u>

As a twenty-year-old car owner, I recently bought car insurance for my new car. I have had no accidents or moving violations. Still, I paid $200 more for the same coverage that my father has.

<u>The **state insurance commission** should investigate this unfair situation and correct it.</u>

1. Dear Editor,

   _____

   _____

       I am an amateur actor. For 15 hours a month, I volunteer my services to a local puppet theater. Every year for the past five years we have put on eight puppet shows for children living in city shelters. This year, because of cuts in federal funding for the arts, we will put on only four shows.

   _____

   _____

2. Dear Editor,

   _____

   _____

       When I was young, I loved to play ball. But I had no place to play. The playgrounds were filthy and dangerous. Then the West Side Center opened. For a small yearly fee, I could play ball every day after school with my friends. Now, the center has a leaky roof that it does not have the money to fix. If the center cannot fix the roof, it will have to close.

   _____

   _____

3. Dear Editor,

   _____

   _____

       Yesterday, a little girl on my block was shot by a bullet during a drive-by shooting. This kind of tragedy has happened three times in the last year. Drug traffic in the area is very high, but I have never seen anyone arrested.

   _____

   _____

Check your answers on page 124.

Separating Your Opinion from the Evidence

Once you have stated your opinion, go on to give evidence to support your opinion. Make sure that you give real evidence and do not simply restate your beliefs in different words. In Example A, the writer has restated the opinion instead of giving his reasons. In Example B, the writer gives two reasons for her opinion.

EXAMPLE A

I think we should not spank children because spanking is bad. It is not a good idea, and so we should not do it.

EXAMPLE B

We should not spank children. Using violence against children teaches them to use violence too. Also, we can lose control while spanking and actually hurt them.

Exercise 8.2

In each of the following items, an opinion is given and then restated. Rewrite the statement and remove the restatement. Then add at least one reason for the opinion. Use Example B as an example.

1. Smoking should be banned in all restaurants because it is the right thing to do.

_____

_____

_____

2. I love dogs because they are wonderful animals.

_____

_____

_____

3. Cheating on your income tax is not like stealing because stealing is different.

_____

_____

_____

4. People should not get divorced because divorce is bad.

_____

_____

_____

5. Abortion is wrong because it is wrong to take the life of an unborn child.

_____

_____

_____

Check your answers on page 124.

Building Support

To effectively support your opinion, your evidence should do the following.
1. Show that you are reasonable, fair-minded, and knowledgeable, and that readers can trust you.
2. Give the numerical facts that support your opinion or request.
3. Give background information that supports your opinion or request.
4. Make an appropriate personal or emotional appeal to the reader.

ESTABLISH TRUST

To believe your writing, your audience must trust you to be fair and reasonable, and to know about your topic. Look at the following letter, which Freda Marino wrote after being awakened at night.

Dear Landlord,

    If you don't get the maniac that lives upstairs
to stop beating those drums, I'm going to sue you
both!

                              Sincerely,

                         Freda Marino
                          Freda Marino

In the morning Freda reread her letter. She realized that because of her angry tone, the landlord might not believe her or might be too annoyed to help her. She saw, too, that describing her neighbor as a "maniac" was not fair. She was attacking him personally instead of objecting to his *actions*.

Freda rewrote the letter. She changed the tone from angry to firm but reasonable. She also included a request, factual evidence of days and times, and personal evidence of how the drumming had affected her.

Dear Landlord,

I would very much appreciate it if you would tell the
tenant who lives in the apartment above me to stop
playing the drums at night.

Every evening for the past two weeks, he has begun
drumming at 7 p.m. and played until midnight. The sound
is very loud and very disturbing. I cannot hear my
television or talk on the telephone. It is impossible
for me to get to sleep.

I have spoken to the tenant three times about playing
more softly and stopping sooner. He ignores me and just
continues the same way.

This tenant is breaking the law by making such noise
after 10 p.m., and he is interfering with my right to
"quiet enjoyment" of my apartment, as my lease states.

I am sure that a few words from you would make a big
difference in this situation.

Thank you for your help.

                              Sincerely,

                         Freda Marino
                          Freda Marino

One way to make your writing more trustworthy is to mention an important outside **authority** (uh-THAHR-uh-tee), or expert, that your reader will respect. The authority can be a person, law, agency, or document. For example, in her letter, Freda notes that the noisy neighbor is breaking the law and interfering with her lease conditions.

Exercise 8.3a

The following statements would make a reader mistrust the writer. Rewrite each statement to be more effective. An example is done for you.

Example: I think that since I could stop biting my nails all by myself, anyone can kick a drug habit.

To kick a drug habit you have to take responsibility for yourself. It may not be easy, but anyone who really wants to should be able to do it.

1. You have to be a depraved murderer to go hunting poor innocent deer.

   _____

   _____

2. Men should never be awarded custody of children. Even a mother who drinks and goes out every night is a more fit parent than any man could be.

   _____

   _____

3. You have done such a lousy repair job on my car that I'm sure it will never run again.

   _____

   _____

4. I don't know anything about teaching math, but I could do better than you did with my son.

   _____

   _____

Check your answers on page 124.

GIVE THE NECESSARY FACTS

Writing is more persuasive if you can include important facts. Make sure to give exact dates, times, places, and names. If you have numerical facts (statistics), provide them in a format that is easy to read. In Example A, the writer has not given the important facts. The letter in Example B is much more persuasive. The writer put in the facts, which are underlined here, and included a copy of the receipt as physical evidence.

EXAMPLE A

Dear Julius Tool Company,

A hammer that I bought was defective. The top flew off when I tried to use it and almost hit my kid in the head!

I'm furious that you sell such shoddy equipment, and I want a replacement right away. If I don't hear from you, I'm calling a lawyer.

Sincerely,

EXAMPLE B

Julius Tool Company

Dear Manager,

Please send me a replacement for a defective Tru-Julius heavy duty hammer. I bought the hammer on April 19 at Lindenbaum Hardware for $14.95 plus tax.

The first time I tried to use the hammer, the head flew off almost striking my child. I noticed that the wooden handle was split.

The store manager instructed me to write to you. A copy of my store receipt is enclosed. I will be happy to send you the broken hammer if you send me postage.

Thank you for your attention.

Sincerely,

Exercise 8.3b

For each thesis, brainstorm a list of the facts that you would need to write a persuasive letter. An example is done for you.

Example: *Thesis:*   To persuade your medical clinic that you have paid all your bills

          Facts: Dates of the clinic appointments

                Dates of the bills

                Amounts of the bills

                Copies of your paid receipts or checks

1. *Thesis:* To persuade a former employer to write a letter recommending you for a job at a new company

   Facts: _____

   _____

   _____

   _____

2. *Thesis:* To persuade your landlord to allow you to sublet your apartment for the summer to your cousin

   Facts: _____

   _____

   _____

   _____

3. *Thesis:* To persuade the city housing department to check your building for housing code violations

   Facts: _____

   _____

   _____

   _____

4. *Thesis:* To persuade the minister at your church that it would be a good
idea to start a support group for young parents

Facts: _____

_____

_____

_____

Check your answers on page 124.

SKILL REVIEW: CAUSE AND EFFECT

You can use cause and effect to present ideas or facts. To be believable, the cause should logically and reasonably lead to the result you give. The cause should not seem too limited or too general for the effect. You can use cause and effect in any kind of writing. Here is an example in a business letter.

Filbert Party Supplies
78541 Flatbush Avenue
Brooklyn, New York 11234

April 2, 199-

Ms. Jan Sherman
4655 West 42nd Street
New York, NY 10016

Dear Ms. Sherman,
We apologize for the delay in filling your order of October 27 for party supplies from our December catalog.

The party favors you requested—Items 75, 81, and 90—were out of stock. We expected a shipment in that day. However, because of the recent blizzards, all airports were closed and our shipment was rerouted.

To show our appreciation for your patience, we are enclosing a box of our specialty foil balloons and an inflator.

Thank you again for your patience.

Sincerely,

Jason Petner

ORGANIZE YOUR EVIDENCE

Choose organizational patterns that fit your evidence.

- Cause and effect. Look at the letter on page 83. The writer showed how the loud drumming had caused negative effects for her.
- Comparison and contrast. Look at Kendra's letter to the editor on page 79. She compared her neighborhood to other neighborhoods to show that it had more of the unwanted projects.

You can also include other forms of writing in your persuasive writing.

- Narrative writing. In the letter to Julius Tool Company on page 85, the writer narrated what happened when he tried to use the hammer.
- Descriptive writing. Freda Marino used descriptive details to create a clear picture of the loud drumming in her letter on page 83.
- Informative writing. The letter to Julius Tool Company on page 85 uses informative writing to present the facts of the hammer purchase.

WRITER'S MODEL: LETTER OF REQUEST

One example of persuasive writing is the **letter of request.** A letter of request asks the reader to give us information or to do something. For routine, everyday requests, as in Example A, the letter should be direct and polite. For more difficult or unusual requests, as in Example B, the letter will have to be very convincing.

A letter of request starts with a business or personal business heading and a standard opening ("Dear —,"). In the first paragraph, state your request politely and clearly. Succeeding paragraphs should give facts and background information that the reader will need. The last paragraph should restate the action you want taken and thank the reader for his or her help.

Example A

Return address and date	75-382 Broadway New York, NY 10027 February 7, 199-
Inside address	Department of Housing 1234 Official Street New York, NY 10000
Salutation	Dear Sir or Madam,
Body supporting details	Please send me a form for reporting repairs needed in my grandmother's apartment.
	The living room wall has been damaged by water and needs to be repaired.
	The damage was caused two weeks ago by a broken pipe in the wall. The pipe has been fixed, but the wall has not been.

Body supporting details	My grandmother, Olivia Suarez, lives in apartment S-45.
Conclusion	If you need to reach me, please call 555-9847.
Closing	Sincerely, *Jaime Suarez* Jaime Suarez

Example B

Return address and date	625 West 87th Street New York, NY 10024 January 6, 199-
Inside address	Parking Violations Bureau 5678 Violations Street New York, NY 10272
Salutation	Dear Sir or Madam:
Request	I would like to plead not guilty to the parking violation indicated on Summons 77-5341-M. I believe I should not have to pay the $35 fine shown on the summons.
Supporting details (narrative)	On the morning of January 5, my car was parked on the south side of West 105th Street at the corner of West End Avenue. The sign said there was no parking between 8 a.m. and 11 a.m. for that day, Thursday. It was 8 a.m. by my watch, when I walked toward my car that morning. The traffic officer was standing by the car. I called out that I was the owner of the car. He answered that he had already begun writing the summons. My seven-year-old son was with me, and I was going to drive him to school. I waited quietly for the officer to finish writing the summons. Then I got into my car and drove off immediately.
Supporting argument	The time on the summons is 8:02. I feel that a two-minute difference between the officer's watch and my own shows some doubt about the facts. Certainly, the fact that I was on the spot as the officer wrote the summons proves that I had planned to obey the parking regulations.
Conclusion	I hope you will agree with me that I was not guilty of violating parking regulations in this situation and that I should not be fined.
Closing	Sincerely, *Otis R. Wilson* Otis R. Wilson
Notice of enclosure	Enclosed: Summons 77-5341-M

Writing Assignments

Building Your Word Power

Add to your word notebook the Key Terms and Life Skill Words from this chapter. Break each word into syllables. Write an original sentence for at least five of the words. Then choose a few of the words and write synonyms for them.

Reading to Write

Read through magazines and newspapers for examples of persuasive writing. Look for editorials, columns, letters to the editor, and op-ed page articles. Clip or photocopy at least two articles, and add them to your portfolio. For each article, write (1) the writer's opinion and (2) the writer's request, if there is one. Underline at least one item of evidence in each article.

Writer's Portfolio Assignment

Choose two topics from those listed below or use two of your own. For each topic, write a brief persuasive paragraph that (1) states an opinion, (2) gives evidence, and (3) gives a summary and request. Keep the paragraphs in your portfolio.

- Should a teenager be able to have an abortion without the consent of her parents?
- Should the government require all eighteen-year-olds to serve two years in the military or in some form of public service?
- Should adopted children have the right to know who their birth parents are?
- Should we stop allowing immigrants into this country?
- Should we make English the official national language?

Chapter 9

Writing Essays on Tests

Hector Ramirez recognized his son Felix's footsteps clambering up the stairs outside of his apartment before he burst through the door.

"It's not fair," Felix said.

Hector sighed. "What isn't fair now?" he asked.

"Why do I have to tie up the newspapers, separate out the cans, and all that?"

"You know," Hector explained, for the ninetieth time, "that's your job. Your sister has her own jobs, too."

"Not Angela. Everybody else. The whole rest of the building just seems to throw things wherever they please."

"Come on, Felix," Hector said, "You know, it's the law now. Everybody has to do the same thing we're doing. Not only that, it's a good thing to do."

"Come see," Felix told his father, "I'll show you what I mean." He took his father's hand and pulled him out of the chair. "Let's go look."

Downstairs in front of the building, Hector saw exactly what Felix meant. It was a mess. It looked as if nobody but Felix had followed the instructions for **recycling.**

"Well, Felix," he told his son, "our neighbors just don't seem to be as responsible as we are. We're going to continue to follow the rules." While he talked, he sighed inwardly, wondering if he was going to have to teach the whole neighborhood **responsibility,** in order to make the world fair for his son.

Key Terms

- analyze
- essay
- essay question

Life Skill Words

- energy
- fraud
- House of Representatives
- landfill
- natural resources
- polls
- recycling
- register
- responsibility
- Senate

Reading the Question

Tests often require students to answer questions in their own words. A long written response, sometimes expressing a point of view, is called an **essay.** Before you can answer an **essay question,** you have to know what is being asked. That sounds simple, but is not always so straightforward. First, sometimes questions are written as though they were statements. Second, a question on an essay test may be a fairly long paragraph. It is your job to identify the topic of the essay and to decide what is required for a correct response.

When you read the question, look for three kinds of information:

1. a topic for the essay
2. general information about that topic
3. instructions for how to answer it

Instructions may include such things as the length of the essay and the specific types of information you should include. You can use key words to help you figure out how you should approach writing your essay.

For example, if a question asks you to *summarize* information, you do not have to give every single detail. A *summary* is a brief retelling of main points.

Many essay questions include the phrase *compare and contrast.* This phrase asks you to describe the similarities and differences between two things. When a question only uses the word *compare,* you should focus on similarities. The word *compare,* however, may also mean "describe differences." Read the whole question carefully and decide if you need to describe differences in order to write a complete answer. When a question only asks you to *contrast,* on the other hand, you should describe differences only.

When a question asks you to **analyze,** you must examine the different aspects of the topic in detail. To analyze means to break a topic into its parts.

When you are asked to state your *opinion,* you should give your own ideas about a subject. Whenever a question asks for your opinion, *support* your point of view with the facts you know about the subject.

Exercise 9.1

Read each of the essay questions below. Underline the topic. Then, on the lines that follow, restate the topic as a question in your own words, and list the instructions for answering the question. The first one is done for you.

1. Voting is a basic right and responsibility of every United States citizen, yet many Americans do not bother to go to the **polls.** Some people believe that making it easier to **register** to vote would help. Others think that making it too easy would lead to **fraud.** Write two or three paragraphs <u>giving your opinion about whether or not registering to vote should be made easier.</u> Back up your opinion with examples from your own experience or from news stories you have read or heard.

   Question: <u>Do you think we should make it easier for people to</u> <u>register to vote?</u>

   Instructions: <u>The essay should give my opinion, should be two or</u> <u>three paragraphs long, and should contain examples from real life</u> <u>and news reports.</u>

2. The United States **Senate** and the **House of Representatives** are two bodies that make up our Congress. Describe the rules about who can run for these two bodies and how long a person serves in a single term. Contrast how these rules affect the way each body works.

   Question: _____

   _____

   Instructions: _____

   _____

3. Many people today have different ideas about the importance of recycling and what its effect could be in the world. A demonstration of the positive effects of recycling may convince people that their efforts would not be wasted. Write two or three paragraphs outlining how recycling everyday products can benefit our world.

   Question: _____

   _____

   Instructions: _____

   _____

4. People have different reasons for returning to school. They also face different problems reaching their educational goals. Think about a person you know (or yourself). Write a three- or four-paragraph essay explaining this person's reasons for going back to school and the problems he or she faced in achieving the goal. Explain why you think this person will (or will not) succeed.

Question: _____

_____

Instructions: _____

_____

5. We admire people because of their good qualities and because of their actions. Choose a person you admire. Write a four-paragraph essay explaining why you admire him or her. Begin with an introductory paragraph that identifies your subject and tells why he or she is worthy of admiration. End with a concluding paragraph that summarizes your reasons and explains what people can learn from your subject's good example.

Question: _____

_____

Instructions: _____

_____

Check your answers on page 124.

SKILL REVIEW: ORGANIZING ESSAYS BY ORDER OF IMPORTANCE

When you use order of importance to organize information, you rank the ideas according to how important they are to your purpose. You can begin with the most important idea, and move from it down to the least important idea; or you can start with the least important idea and build up to the most important one. This form of organization is very effective when your purpose is to state an opinion or to persuade readers to do something.

Building a paragraph from your least important idea to your strongest idea allows you to save your most persuasive argument for last and leaves a strong impression on the readers mind. Going in the other direction is usually less effective. However, it does allow you to begin your discussion forcefully.

Timing Your Writing

You may write essays as homework or for your own satisfaction. When you write an essay on a test, however, you must plan carefully so you can complete your work within a limited amount of time. Therefore, it is a good idea to read through all the test essay questions quickly, and make a rough schedule for answering them. Allow the most time for the hardest questions, or the ones worth the most points. For example, if you are given one hour to write one long essay and two short essays, leave 30 minutes to write the long essay and 15 minutes to write each short one. Watch the time closely, and at the end of each time period, move on to the next essay.

Because of time pressures, you may be tempted to jump right in and start writing your answer to the first question immediately. Resist this temptation. Spending a little time to prepare your answers is worthwhile because the writing itself will go more smoothly. In other words, even when taking a test, you should follow the steps in the writing process. You will, of course, have to follow the steps in a shortened way. Begin the prewriting stage by gathering your ideas. Jot down your thoughts on a scrap of paper. Do not necessarily go with the first thoughts that enter your mind. Rather, allow yourself a few extra seconds to brainstorm for additional ideas. When you are finished, organize the ideas by numbering them in the order that you want to cover them. Cross out any points that you decide are not relevant. You may rewrite your ideas into a short outline. Time spent organizing will save you time in the long run.

Once you have organized your thoughts, you are ready to start writing. It's a good idea to begin with a sentence or two that restates the topic from the question. This will help you focus on the information required for a complete answer.

Exercise 9.2a

Choose two essay questions from Exercise 9.1. On a separate piece of paper, jot down as many ideas as you can for an essay on this topic. Allow yourself one minute to do this.

When you have finished, take another minute to cross out ideas you think are not relevant to the topic, and number the remaining ideas in the order you would like to use them. Write those ideas in order on the lines below. The example from Exercise 9.1 is developed for you.

Example: Registering to vote should be easier.

You're not represented if you don't vote, and that's not democratic.

Poor people are less likely to vote than rich people when it's hard to register.

Some people now don't know how to register.

We can still have procedures to protect against fraud.

1. Ideas for Essay 1

_____

_____

_____

_____

2. Ideas for Essay 2

_____

_____

_____

_____

Exercise 9.2b

Using your ideas from Exercise 9.2a, write a topic sentence for two essays. Allow yourself no more than two minutes to come up with each sentence. Remember to use the original questions from Exercise 9.1 as guides when you formulate these sentences. A topic sentence for the example in Exercise 9.1 is done for you.

Example: <u>I believe that registering to vote should be made easier.</u>

1._____

_____

_____

_____

2._____

_____

_____

_____

Writing a Timed Essay

It can be a challenge to get all your ideas down clearly before time runs out. Follow these suggestions to keep yourself on target.

- Budget time for writing each essay and for revising and editing them, too.
- Skip lines as you write and leave wide margins. You can use this extra space when you revise and edit your essays.
- Stick to your outline or organized list for each essay.
- If you think of a great idea while you are writing, add it to your outline. Continue writing the current paragraph, though.
- Try to spell words correctly as you write, but don't waste time. If you are not sure of a spelling, write "sp?" above the word, and check it later.
- Check your time as you work. Move on to the next essay as soon as you can.
- Leave a small amount of time to reread, revise, and edit your work. You can move a sentence by circling it and drawing an arrow. You can add a word or sentence on the blank lines you left. Cross out unneeded words with a single line.

Exercise 9.3

Give yourself 30 minutes to write essays on the two topics you used in Exercises 9.2a and b. Allow yourself one or two minutes to review your outline and topic sentence for each essay. Then allow yourself eight or nine minutes to write each essay. Finally, allow yourself four or five minutes to revise and edit each essay. Use two separate sheets of paper and include both essays in your Portfolio.

WRITER'S MODEL: LETTER TO THE EDITOR

Most letters to the editor are written to convince readers of the newspaper to share an opinion. It is important for the letter to be brief and well organized. You should state your arguments in a logical way and back them up with facts and examples. The following model shows you some of the characteristics of a letter to the editor.

```
To the Editor:
I am distressed to find that many people in our town are
not following the rules for recycling. It takes very
little extra effort to bundle newspapers and separate cans
```

---

and bottles for recycling. The benefits of doing so, however, are great.

Recycling saves precious **natural resources,** it decreases the use of **energy,** and it slows the rate at which our **landfills** are used up. In addition, following the rules makes our town a nicer place to live and sets an important example for our children.

                              Hector Ramirez
                              Springbrook Center

In this example, Hector writes to the editor to express his opinion that people throughout the community should follow the rules for recycling. Notice that the first paragraph states the writer's opinion, and the second paragraph gives support. The last sentence also serves as a conclusion.

Writing Assignments

Reading to Write

Choose an article from your local newspaper about a current event important to you as a member of the community. Suppose that you were a teacher giving an essay test about the events covered in the newspaper article. Write at least one essay question you could ask that would get at the most important issues involved in the event covered by the article. Your essay question should include some background information, a statement of the essay topic, and instructions about how the test takers should go about writing their answers.

Writer's Portfolio Assignment

1. On a separate paper, write an essay to answer the question you wrote for Reading to Write above. Allow yourself three minutes to organize your essay. Allow yourself ten minutes to draft your essay. Allow yourself an additional two minutes to reread your answer and correct any errors or make other improvements.

2. Choose a community issue about which you have a strong opinion. It might have to do with the way schools in your town are run, traffic conditions, or a safety concern, for example. Write a letter to the editor stating your opinion. Jot down your ideas before you begin, and arrange them in a way that you think will make your case most effectively. Use Hector's letter to the editor on this page as a model.

Chapter 10

Revising Structure and Wording

Melanie Chung pored over the **want ads** while she ate her cereal. She had been staying at cousin Richard's for three weeks, and she still had no job.

"Maybe I should go home," she said to Richard.

"But we agreed that you had a better chance of getting a job here," he replied.

"I'm imposing on you," Melanie went on. "I answer the ads that are right for me but never get the job."

"I'm sure your luck will change," Richard's wife, Mai, reassured Melanie. "Anyway, you're a big help with the kids."

The family then read the Sunday paper in silence.

"Listen," Richard said. "MaxMart has bought the old mill on Twentieth Street to make into a super store. They're going to need experienced salespeople. Why don't you write them?"

Melanie grinned. She would find their address at the library and send them a **resume** and **cover letter.** This time she would beat the crowd and get the job.

Key Terms

- completeness
- dangling modifier
- emphasis
- misplaced modifier
- order
- synonym
- transition
- unity
- wordiness

Life Skill Words

- administrative assistant
- cover letter
- performance appraisal
- qualifications
- resume
- retail
- salesmanship
- want ads

Reviewing Audience, Purpose, and Basic Structure

Lesson 1

As you learned in Chapter 1, **revising** is the process of reviewing what you have written to make it more effective. Before looking at your draft, take some time to think about your audience and purpose. Remember, the effectiveness of your writing depends on how well it communicates your purpose to your audience. Then look at the structure of your essay as a whole. Remember that essays have three main parts: the introduction, body, and conclusion. The introduction should grab the reader's attention and state the topic of the essay. The body should contain paragraphs with facts, examples, and ideas that support, develop, and explain the topic. The conclusion should restate the topic, summarize the ideas, and tie the essay together. In addition to checking these parts, make sure that your essay contains smooth **transitions,** or links, between paragraphs that present new ideas.

Looking at Unity, Order, Completeness, and Emphasis

Lesson 2

Each paragraph in your essay should have unity, order, and completeness. You should also be sure that the emphasis of each paragraph suits your purpose.

A paragraph has **unity** when every idea relates to the topic and purpose. You want to avoid irrelevant ideas that will confuse your readers and distract them from your purpose. You can check for unity by asking, Did I include only information that is on the topic?

Order has to do with how you arrange ideas. Check that the ideas in the paragraph follow each other in a logical way. You can check for order by asking, Did I arrange the ideas in a logical way?

Completeness means including all essential information. You can check for completeness by asking, Have I included everything readers need to know?

Emphasis is the amount of stress that you give each idea. Make sure the most important idea is given the most stress. You might do this by putting it first—or by saving it for last. Give more support to important ideas. Support less important ideas with fewer details. You can check for emphasis by asking, Will my readers know which ideas are most important?

Exercise 10.2a

The paragraphs below are from cover letters that job seekers sent with their resumes. The purpose of a cover letter is to convince an employer to consider you for a job.

If a paragraph has unity, write OK on the line. If it does not, write X on the line. Then cross out the idea, or ideas, that do not belong. The first one is done for you.

__X__ 1. I am writing to answer your ad for a **retail** sales clerk. As you will learn from the enclosed resume, I majored in retailing in high school. For the past three years, I have worked in the toy department at Thompson and Smith's. ~~While I was in school, I worked part-time as a file clerk at Quasada, Inc.~~ I am now enrolled in a **salesmanship** course at Independence Community College.

_____ 2. I believe you will find me highly qualified for the position of **administrative assistant.** I have good typing and computer skills, and I take shorthand. I am also extremely well organized and enjoy doing office work.

_____ 3. Although I have never worked in a nursery school before, I would make an excellent teaching aide. I raised four children of my own, staying home in order to be a full-time mother. During those years, I enjoyed all my household responsibilities and became an excellent cook and baker. I sell my cakes to friends and neighbors when they give parties. I was also active in the PTA and often volunteered to chaperon class trips. After the children were grown, I worked as a school crossing guard, where my entire effort was dedicated to the safety of children.

Check your answers on page 125.

Exercise 10.2b

Each of the paragraphs below is written by an employee who wants to inform a supervisor about something. The sentences in each paragraph are numbered. If the ideas are presented in good order, write OK on the line below. If not, show how you would rearrange the sentences by writing the sentence numbers in a new order. The first one is done for you.

1. (1) I will be leaving on October 31. (2) I have accepted a job at Santori Hardware Store. (3) Not only does this position offer me more money, but I will sell products that really interest me. (4) At Santori's I will be selling the tools I so enjoy using. (5) I have always been something of a Do-It-Yourselfer. (6) I will be sorry to leave Leston's and will miss working with you. (7) Before I leave, I will make sure that the other clerks have all the information they need to get along without me.

   __2, 1, 3, 5, 4, 6, 7__

Revising Structure and Wording

101

2. (1) I called Rapaport's this morning to find out what happened to the envelopes we ordered. (2) He told me he could fill the order immediately if I faxed him a copy of our purchase order. (3) The person I spoke to had no record of our order. (4) Then we would have the envelopes by the end of the week. (5) I followed up by faxing the order, so you can expect the envelopes by Friday.

_____

3. (1) Here is the information about vacation preferences you asked for. (2) Mary and Joanna would both like to go away during the first part of June. (3) Harold does not want to take his vacation until after Labor Day. (4) Chee wants to take his vacation from June 16 to June 30. (5) Neither Andrea nor Tony have any plans, and they would be happy to work their schedules around other people's. (6) I would like to go away the last two weeks in July.

_____

Check your answers on page 125.

Exercise 10.2c

Each of the paragraphs below was written by an employee to inform a supervisor about something. Decide if the material is complete. (Will the reader have all the necessary information?) Then answer the question below. The first one is done for you.

1. While I was cleaning the display shelves this morning, I noticed that one of them was quite shaky. When I looked closer I found that a screw was missing from the bracket that holds the shelf to the wall. If the screw is not replaced, the shelf may fall down. This would lead to damaged merchandise. More importantly, if anybody is standing near the shelf when it falls, it may lead to serious injury. Can you get the maintenance department to fix the shelf as soon as possible?

   Does the reader have all the information needed? If not, what is missing?
   <u>No, the writer did not tell where the shelf with the missing screw is located.</u>

2. Friday is Beth's last day before her maternity leave. Some of us are planning a shower for her. We would like you to come. We have reserved the fourth-floor conference room, and we are all chipping in for a cake. And, of course, we each plan to bring a small present—something practical.

   Does the reader have all the information needed? If not, what is missing?

   _____

   _____

3. Here is my expense report for my trip to the plant last week. Could you please sign it and forward it to the accounting department? They need it by the end of the month.

   Does the reader have all the information needed? If not, what is missing?

   _____

   _____

Check your answers on page 125.

Exercise 10.2d

Each of the paragraphs below was written by an employee in order to convince a supervisor to do something. Think about whether each writer has emphasized the most important idea. Then answer the questions that follow. The first one is done for you.

1. I have been working at Galaxy Supply Company for over a year, and I have not yet been given a raise. Most people get a raise after one year, so I think it's time for me to get one. You told me in my last **performance appraisal** that my work was very good. You said I will have a future at Galaxy. Now my rent is going up, and with the new baby, I have child-care expenses that I did not have before, so I really need more money. I hope you will give me a raise.

What idea is most important? <u>The idea that the writer is good at the job and has a future at Galaxy.</u>

Has the writer emphasized this idea? Explain your answer. <u>No, the idea is buried among points that are less important to the supervisor.</u>

2. I would like to take a course in bookkeeping. I know the company pays tuition for courses that will improve job performance when a supervisor approves. The bookkeeping course should help me do a better job. Since the course doesn't meet until 8 p.m., taking it will not interfere with my work, and I will even be able to continue working overtime. I hope you will approve this course since I know it will make me a better employee.

What idea is the most important? _____

_____

Has the writer emphasized this idea? Explain your answer. _____

_____

_____

3. The lines at the checkout counter get very long every day in the late afternoon. On Saturdays they are even longer. I have noticed that customers get cross when they wait too long. Some of them even say they will not come back to Rawlson's Market. I think it would be worth having some of the stock clerks act as baggers, or maybe even hiring one or two more part-time people to do bagging during the busy times.

What idea is the most important? _____

_____

Has the writer emphasized this idea? Explain your answer. _____

_____

_____

Check your answers on page 125.

Revising Structure and Wording

Choosing the Best Words

After you have checked your writing for structure, unity, order, completeness, and emphasis, it is time to focus on the words you have chosen. Think about whether you used the words that mean exactly what you intend. Most words have a number of **synonyms,** words that mean the same or almost the same thing. Some of these words are more specific than others. For example, *noise* is a general word. *Screech, whistle, echo,* and *thud* are specific words.

   If you think a word is not exactly right, brainstorm for a better one. If brainstorming does not help, turn to a dictionary, which has some synonyms, or thesaurus, which has many more. Be careful when you choose a synonym, however. You may be tempted to pick one that sounds fancy and will impress people. Be sure you know what a word means before you use it. Remember, you are looking for a word that *means* what you want to say.

Exercise 10.3

Think of a specific word to replace the underlined general word in each sentence. Write the word on the line. (Together, the sentences make up a complete paragraph, so read them all before you begin.) The first one has been done for you.

1. Many <u>people</u> dislike our new automatic phone system. ___customers___

2. Some of them <u>tell</u> about having to listen to so many choices. _____

3. Others say that the recorded voice is <u>bad</u>. _____

4. One customer told me that pushing all those buttons made her finger <u>hurt</u>.

   _____

5. They all agree that human beings are <u>nicer</u> than machines. _____

Check your answers on page 125.

SKILL REVIEW: PUTTING MODIFIERS WHERE THEY BELONG

Phrases, clauses, or single words can act as adjectives or adverbs. Sometimes these modifiers seem to apply to the wrong words, though. This often happens when modifiers are misplaced. **Misplaced modifiers** make it difficult for readers to understand what you have written. **Revise** your work to place modifiers as close as possible to the words they modify.

Wrong Meaning	I sold three dresses to a customer from India.
Correct	I sold three dresses from India to a customer.

The first sentence seems fine, *except* the dresses were from India, and not the customer. It can be corrected by putting "from India" next to "dresses."

When you place a modifier between two words, your reader may be unsure of your meaning.

Confusing	We give a 10 percent discount only to senior citizens.
Clear	We give a 10 percent discount to senior citizens only.

Does the first sentence mean that the senior citizens get only 10 percent off while other customers get more? Or are only senior citizens entitled to a discount? The second sentence makes the meaning clear.

When a sentence begins with a phrase, be sure that it logically applies to the subject of the sentence. Otherwise it may be a **dangling modifier.**

Wrong	Carrying a pile of suits, the clerk's foot tripped on the step.
Right	Carrying a pile of suits, the clerk caught her foot on the steps.

In the first sentence, did the clerk's foot carry the suits all by itself? The second sentence makes the clerk its subject, so we clearly know who was carrying the suits.

Avoiding Wordiness and Repetition

When you revise, you should not only use the best words, you should also make sure you do not use too many of them. Similarly, you should avoid repeating the same words. Using more words than you need is called **wordiness.** For example:

Wordy	We can *combine* these reports *together* in one folder.
Better	We can *combine* these reports in one folder.

The expression *combine . . . together* is wordy. Since *combining* means *putting together*, only the word *combine* is needed.

Using the same word many times is called repetition. Repetition makes your writing uninteresting. Try to avoid using the same verb again and again, as in this paragraph:

> I *can* type 70 words per minute. I *can* take dictation at 120 words per minute, and I *can* work a fax machine.

Also avoid repeating the same adjective. Don't describe everything as *pretty* or *nice.* You can get rid of repetition by using the same techniques that you used to find more precise words, that is by brainstorming or by using a dictionary or thesaurus.

Exercise 10.4a

Cross out any unnecessary words in these sentences. The first one is done you.

1. From now on, I'm going ~~to try~~ to attempt to get to work on time. (Note: *to attempt* could have been crossed out instead.)

2. In my opinion, I think it would be a good idea if everybody submitted status reports every week.

3. In a modern office of today, the computer has replaced the typewriter, the adding machine, and many other office machines of the past.

4. The maintenance department promised to send someone up tomorrow morning before noon to fix the photocopy machine.

5. As a rule, all members of the staff should always wear safety goggles when operating drills.

6. The constant hum from the fluorescent lights is barely audible to my ears, but it is still annoying anyway.

Check your answers on page 125.

Exercise 10.4b

The following paragraphs are from letters written after job interviews. On separate paper, revise each one to eliminate repetition. The first one has been done for you.

1. I enjoyed talking to you last week about the job opening at MaxMart. I would consider getting the chance to work there a great opportunity. I enjoy selling, and I enjoy working with people. It would be great to be able to do this at a great store like MaxMart.

Possible answer (changes in italics): I *was pleased* to talk to you last week about the job opening at MaxMart. I would consider getting the chance to work there a great opportunity. I *like* selling, and I enjoy working with people. It would be *exciting* to be able to do this at a *wonderful* store like MaxMart.

2. It was nice of you to meet with me last week and discuss the job opening at your company. I would very much like to work there. I like the way you rotate jobs so that everybody gets to learn the whole process. It will be nice for me to know all the jobs involved with baking bread. I like having the chance to learn as much as possible.

3. Although I have never worked in an office before, I think I can do the job successfully. I took typing and shorthand in high school. I took a course in computer programming after I graduated from the community college. When I took a tour of your office last week, I saw that you had the same kind of computer I took my course on, so I should feel quite at home in your office.

Check your answers on page 126.

WRITER'S MODEL: RESUME

A resume is an important job hunting tool. It gives prospective employers an overview of your **qualifications** for a job. Some resumes also include a list of skills. Below is a model resume.

Melanie Chung

675 Weaver Street   Worcester, MA 01601   (617) 555-6740

Objective:	A sales position in a retail store
Experience:	
1993-199- Sales Clerk	Jessica's Gift Shop, 1735 Main Street, Sturbridge, MA 01566 Waited on customers, handled cash register, arranged merchandise displays, helped owner make decisions about what merchandise to carry.
1990-1992 Sales Clerk	Fashion Fair, West Street Mall, Sturbridge, MA 01566 Waited on customers, gave fashion advice, assisted at cashier station.
Education:	Valley Community Adult Education Program, 1991-present Central High School, North Brookfield, MA 05135, completed 10th grade, 1982
References:	Jessica Alvin, owner of Jessica's Gift Shop, 1735 Main Street, Sturbridge, MA 01566. Joanne Torez, assistant manager, Fashion Fair, West Street Mall, Sturbridge, MA 01566.

A CHECKLIST FOR REVISING YOUR WRITING

Structure	Do I present an introductory paragraph, supporting body paragraphs, and a concluding paragraph?
Audience and Purpose	Do I achieve my purpose for my audience?
Unity	Do I include only information that is on the topic?
Order	Do I arrange the ideas in a logical way?
Completeness	Have I included everything readers need to know?
Emphasis	Will my readers know which ideas are most important?
Word Choice	Do I use the specific words I mean?
Wordiness	Do I avoid repetition?
Modifiers	Do my adjectives and adverbs clearly modify the words I intend?

Writing Assignments

Reading to Write

Clip a newspaper want ad for a job you might enjoy. Then write a cover letter you could use if you were sending in your resume. Your purpose is to get the reader to consider you for the job. Use the Writer's Model in Chapter 8 as a guide to the form of a business letter. After you have drafted the letter, put it aside for a few days, then revise it.

Writer's Portfolio Assignment

Choose two pieces of writing from your Writing Portfolio. Revise them by following the steps outlined in this chapter.

Chapter 11

Editing

When Janet Alexander arrived at work, she was surprised to see a note taped to the back of her chair. Mr. Franklin, the head of the **order fulfillment** department, had written "Please see me as soon as you come in."

Janet looked at her watch. It was almost five minutes to nine. "Thank goodness I'm not late," she thought to herself. "In fact, if I hurry, I can show him that I was here early." She quickly put her coat in the closet, grabbed a notebook and pen, and hurried to Mr. Franklin's office.

"Good morning, Mr. Franklin," said Janet with a smile. She hoped she hadn't done anything wrong.

"Good morning, Janet. It's nice to see you're here so promptly. I need your help on a project," Mr. Franklin said. "It's come to my attention that we have a **backlog** on orders in your department. Your supervisor, Ms. McGraw, called me at home last night to say she's going to be out recovering from her surgery for at least another ten days. I want you to figure out what's going on before our busy season starts in a couple of weeks. You'll need to meet with the members of your department and write a report on why orders are backing up."

"I see," said Janet. She was very flattered at being given this assignment, but she also felt very nervous. "Is there anything specific that you want me to look for?" She hoped this was the right question to ask.

"Just give me your **analysis** of the problem. Break it down into parts and tell me what you and the staff think we can do to solve it. Today is Monday, so I'd like your report by a week from today." Mr. Franklin stood and Janet realized the meeting was over.

As Janet walked out, her mind was spinning. She realized that she would have to prove herself with this report. What a challenge!

Key Terms

- editing
- mechanics
- proofreading
- proofreading symbols

Life Skills Words

- analysis
- backlog
- order fulfillment

REVIEW OF RULES

Editing means doing a final check of your written work to make sure it is completely correct. At this stage in the writing process you check your sentences, usage, spelling, capitalization, and punctuation. Editing your work is important because errors distract the reader's attention from your message. They may confuse the reader or make the reader feel that he or she cannot trust what you are saying. No matter how good the content of your writing is, you will be judged poorly if your written work is filled with mistakes.

Proofreading is the slow and careful process of reading your revised work and marking errors for correction.

Complete Sentences

When you edit your work, check each sentence for completeness. A complete sentence must contain both a subject, a verb, and often, a thought completer. It must form a single complete thought. When you are putting your ideas on paper, it is easy to run sentences together or write sentence fragments without realizing it.

RUN-ON SENTENCES

Do any of your sentences have two complete thoughts run together without punctuation? Have you used a comma without a conjunction to join two clauses? If so, this is a run-on sentence that needs to be broken into two sentences.

Incorrect: Christmas is our busy season, each year it seems to start earlier than the year before.

Correct: Christmas is our busy season. Each year it seems to start earlier than the year before.

SENTENCE FRAGMENTS

Does each sentence have a subject and a verb? Does it express a complete thought? If a sentence does not have both a subject and a verb it is a sentence fragment and needs to be corrected.

Incorrect: The season used to start around mid-November. Never before Halloween.

Correct: The season used to start around mid-November. It never began before Halloween.

Correct: The season used to start around mid-November—never before Halloween.

Exercise 11.1

Find any sentence fragments or run-on sentences in the following paragraph. Rewrite them in the spaces below to make them complete sentences. If a sentence is correct, write *correct* in the space.

```
TO:       Otis Franklin, Director, Order Fulfillment
FROM:     Janet Alexander, Order Fulfillment Clerk
DATE:     November 3, 199—
SUBJECT:  Report on Order Backlog
```

(1) As you requested, I met with the order fulfillment staff to discuss our recent problem with back orders we reviewed the backlog records for the past eight weeks. (2) In the past four weeks, back orders have averaged about 50 per week. (3) About 35 more per week than usual.

(4) We found two specific reasons for this problem, first, one staff member was assigned temporary duty in the Inventory Department. (5) Due to an emergency. (6) Second, orders overall have increased by about 10 percent the sales office says Christmas orders are coming in earlier than usual.

1. _____

   _____

2. _____

   _____

3. _____

   _____

4. _____

   _____

5. _____

   _____

6. _____

   _____

Check your answers on page 126.

Editing

Lesson 2

Correct Usage

Look at each sentence part and make sure that you have used the correct forms of verbs, pronouns, adjectives, and adverbs.

VERBS

Are verbs in the correct tense? As you read through your entire piece make sure you have not shifted from one tense to another, unless it clearly makes sense to do so. Check to see that verbs agree with their subject in number.

Incorrect:	In the last month orders has been delayed, but we will have a solution soon.
Correct:	In the last month orders have been delayed, but we will have a solution soon.

Exercise 11.2a

The following paragraph contains errors in verb usage. Cross out each verb that is used incorrectly and write the correct verb form above the incorrect word.

Dear Customer:

Armstrong Manufacturing is delighted that you had placed your order for Christmas packaging before the rush. This mean that you are expecting a busy season, which are good for everyone. We wants to let you know that your order are being processed. Due to the large number of early orders we have receive this year, our fulfillment time have increased slightly. This letter is to assure you that your order will have been processed within the next five days.

Check your answers on page 126.

PRONOUNS

Do pronouns agree in gender and number with the nouns to which they
refer? Are pronouns in the correct form? Make sure that subject
(nominative case) pronouns are used to refer to subjects and that object
(objective case) pronouns are used to refer to objects.

Incorrect: Mr. Franklin asked me to send copies of the report to he and
                       Ms. McGraw.

Correct: Mr. Franklin asked me to send copies of the report to him and
                       Ms. McGraw.

To him and Ms. McGraw is a prepositional phrase. The objective pronoun
him is used as an object of the preposition.

Exercise 11.2b

In the following paragraph, fill in the blank spaces with a correct pronoun form.

```
TO:        Order Fulfillment Clerks
FROM:      Janet Alexander
DATE:      November 3, 199—
SUBJECT:   Order Backlog
```

(1) Ms. McGraw has informed Mr. Franklin that

_____ will be out of the office for another

ten days because of _____ surgery. (2) He

asked _____ to meet with _____ to

discuss the problems _____ are having with

backlogged orders. (3) Will each of _____

please review _____ backlog records for the

past eight weeks? (4) Total the number of back orders

and note when _____ started to increase.

(5) _____ will meet tomorrow morning at 10

a.m. in Ms. McGraw's office to discuss this problem.

Check your answers on page 126.

MODIFIERS

Are adjectives used correctly to modify nouns and pronouns? Are adverbs used correctly to modify verbs, adjectives, and other adverbs? Make sure you have not confused one type of modifier with another or used an incorrect comparative form.

Incorrect: Angela has been an order fulfillment clerk for only six months, but she learned the job very quick.

Correct: Angela has been an order fulfillment clerk for only six months, but she learned the job very quickly.

Incorrect: Janet was asked to do the report because she is the most fastest worker on the staff.

Correct: Janet was asked to do the report because she is the fastest worker on the staff.

Exercise 11.2c

In the following paragraph, select the correct form of the adjective or adverb and write it in the blank.

Notice to Order Fulfillment Staff

(1) Some of you seem to be unaware that several of last year's Christmas packaging options sold (poor/poorly) _____. (2) (3) Customers seem to prefer the (traditional/traditionally) _____ colors to some of the (pretty, prettier, prettiest) _____ new colors we introduced last year.

(4) Stock is running (low/lowly) _____ on the new colors because they will not be continued.

(5) Customers may place (special/specially) _____ orders, if they are willing to allow two weeks for delivery. (6) Please notify your (best, better, bestest) _____ customers of this change.

Check your answers on page 126.

Mechanics

Checking for mechanics should be your last editing task. **Mechanics** includes capitalization, punctuation, and spelling. This is the final polish on your writing and it requires a keen eye for detail.

There are three types of mechanical errors to look for. It is best if you read your work three times, checking for each one separately.

CAPITALIZATION

Do all sentences begin with a capital letter? Are all proper nouns capitalized? Are any words incorrectly capitalized?

Incorrect:	Our Company is located in the Diamond building, next to city hall.
Correct:	Our company is located in the Diamond Building, next to City Hall.

PUNCTUATION

Punctuation marks help your writing flow smoothly. They make your message clear by providing signals to the reader. They tell the reader when to pause and when to stop.

- Make sure each sentence has a proper ending punctuation mark (period, question mark, or exclamation point).
- Use colons (:) and semicolons (;) correctly.
- Place commas correctly between parts of sentences and with items listed in a series.

MISSPELLED WORDS

Of all the errors you might make, readers are least patient with spelling errors. People tend to think that spelling errors are the result of stupidity or carelessness. If you are unsure of a spelling look up the word in the dictionary. If you find that you tend to overlook misspellings, try reading each sentence backwards. This technique forces your eyes to focus on one word at a time. It is also a good idea to ask someone else to read the final copy of your work.

Exercise 11.3

The following memo contains errors in capitalization and punctuation. On a separate sheet of paper, rewrite the memo correctly.

```
TO:        Order Fulfillment clerks
FROM:      Otis Franklin, Director, order fulfillment
DATE:      November 12, 199—
SUBJECT:   Cleaning Up The Order Backlog
```

Thank you for your cooperation with Janet in Ms. McGraw's absents. her report has helped me find some soltions to the backlog problem. As of november 15 i will be adding a new Inventory Clerk to the staff of the Inventory Department. Temporarily until the end of the Christmas Seasen this person will work in the Order Fulfillment Department. I will be asking Tamkio to take charge of training the new employee?

Until December 22 yur Department will work overtime on Mondays Wednesdays and Fridays. a schedule will be posted on the bulletin board. Please let me know if you unplanned overtime will be a problem for any of you?

Check your answers on page 126.

WRITERS MODEL: A BUSINESS MEMO

A memo, or memorandum, is a written communication used within an organization. Many companies use a preprinted form.

Janet's report to Mr. Franklin is a good example of standard memo format. The *TO:* and *FROM:* lines identify the correspondents. The *SUBJECT:* line summarizes the topic of the memo.

Notice that Janet's report presents information in a businesslike way. She begins with a statement of the topic and her purpose. In her first sentence she also reminds the reader of their previous discussion. The reader immediately knows what to expect. She then explains the problem. The second paragraph provides the detailed reasons for the backlog problem.

Headings	TO:	Otis Franklin, Director, Order Fulfillment	Include position and department of correspondents
	FROM:	Janet Alexander, Order Fulfillment Clerk	
	DATE:	November 3, 199-	
	SUBJECT:	Report of Order Backlog	Use a simple description

Further define the subject or problem

As you requested, I met with the order fulfillment staff to discuss our recent problem with back orders. We reviewed the backlog records for the past eight weeks. In the past four weeks back orders have averaged about 50 per week, about 35 more per week than usual.

Present explanation or supporting detials

We found two specific reasons for this problem. First, one staff member was assigned temporary duty in the Inventory Department due to an emergency. Second, orders overall have increased by about 10 percent. The sales office says Christmas orders are coming in earlier than usual.

(Missing: Conclusions, suggested solutions, or next steps)

Editing Your Portfolio

Learning to edit and proofread your written work is an ongoing process. You will improve with practice. Proofread your work each and every time you write. Read the following editing guidelines and use the ones that work best for you.

EDITING GUIDELINES

1. When you finish the revision stage of your writing, set it aside for a period of time. If you can, wait until the next day to do your editing. Time away from your written piece helps you see it in a fresh light.

2. Read the entire piece once straight through and look for obvious errors. Mark these with a colored pen or pencil. Then go back and read backward or look at each sentence slowly to find additional errors.

3. Read your work aloud. Often your ears work better than your eyes to pick up incorrect tenses, subject-verb disagreement, or awkward and unclear sentences.

4. Read the piece several times, looking for one type of error in each reading.

5. Ask a friend, relative, or classmate to read your piece and help you look for errors.

6. Make notes of the kinds of errors you make most often and write a personal editing checklist. Keep this checklist in your notebook and refer to it when you are editing. Include words that you most often misspell.

7. Use proofreading symbols to mark your errors. **Proofreading symbols** are standard marks used by professional writers and editors to show corrections in written copy. Proofreading symbols are used in many businesses. Practicing the use of these marks will give you a skill that you can use in the workplace.

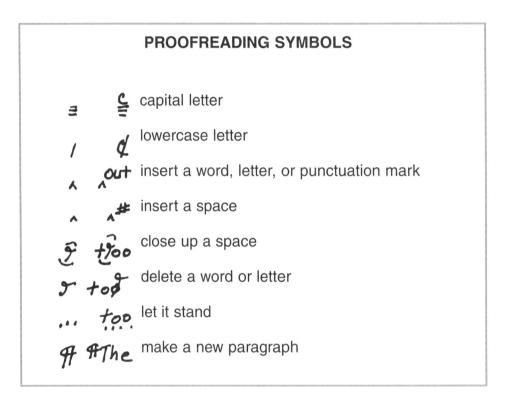

PROOFREADING SYMBOLS

capital letter

lowercase letter

insert a word, letter, or punctuation mark

insert a space

close up a space

delete a word or letter

let it stand

make a new paragraph

Exercise 11.4

Select two long pieces from your Writer's Portfolio. Edit each portfolio piece using the guidelines in this chapter.

Building Your Word Power

Write the Key Terms and Life Skill Words listed in the beginning of this chapter in your notebook. Break each word into syllables.

Reading to Write

Review the draft and final versions of your portfolio assignments. Look for the types of errors that you made repeatedly in your writing. Make a list of these errors and use them to develop a personalized editing checklist.

Writer's Portfolio Assignment

As Jane Alexander, write a follow-up memo to Mr. Franklin on the subject of possible solutions to the problem presented in the Writer's Model memo of November 3. Date the memo November 5, 199-.

A n s w e r   K e y

Chapter 1

Exercise 1.1

1. Topic: Why you should dress like your boss
   Writer's Purpose: persuasive
2. Topic: Why you should check care instructions before buying clothing
   Writer's Purpose: persuasive, informative
3. Topic: Seeing my boss in the clothing department
   Writer's Purpose: narrative
4. Topic: The features of a good pair of work shoes
   Writer's Purpose: descriptive, informative
5. Topic: The reasons for cost differences in shoes
   Writer's Purpose: informative
6. Topic: The proper way to select shoes for fit
   Writer's Purpose: informative

Exercise 1.2a

Answers will vary.
1. Style: probably formal
   Purpose: informative
   Outcome(s):   cleaner, longer-wearing, better-looking baby clothing
2. Style: formal
   Purpose: persuasive, narrative, descriptive
   Outcome(s):   recognition of excellent service
3. Style: informal
   Purpose: descriptive
   Outcome(s):   the friend will look at his or her own shoes in a new way
4. Style: informal
   Purpose: narrative
   Outcome(s):   amusement

Exercise 1.2b

Answers will vary. Be sure that your details match the audience, purpose, and outcomes that you chose in Exercise 1.2a.

Exercise 1.3a

X You might be tempted to write one very long paragraph. <u>Breaking your thoughts into several smaller parts, however, has advantages for both you and your reader.</u> *X* <u>Using short paragraphs makes the writer's job easier.</u> Short paragraphs let you easily check that you covered each idea thoroughly. You will notice if you are mixing ideas together, or if you are leaving out something important. *X* <u>Short paragraphs are also easier to understand.</u> Your readers will be able to concentrate on one idea at a time. They will also know that you intend a new idea to begin with each bite-sized paragraph.

Exercise 1.3b

Answers will vary.
1. More: What is down? What are the other advantages of synthetic-filled coats over down?
2. More: What problems can you have when you wash everything together? How are you supposed to wash colors? whites? delicates?
3. More: What happened next? What did Liza say? Did Shantell buy the dress? Did she feel better? Does she always buy stuff when she's down?
4. More: Give some examples of fad styles that Tom might have. Why are fad styles so important to Tom? Why doesn't Tom get rid of the fad clothing that he no longer wants to wear?

Exercise 1.4

1. revising
2. editing
3. publishing
4. prewriting
5. prewriting
6. revising
7. drafting
8. prewriting
9. drafting
10. editing

Chapter 2

Exercise 2.4

Answers will vary. Sample answer:
1. I. Introduction: Comparison shopping is a way to save money.
   II. Shop around at various kinds of stores
   III. Look for bargains in catalogs.
   IV. Look for information on prices.
   V. Talk to people about where to find bargains and sales.
   VI. Conclusion
2. *Answers will vary.* No suggested answers.

Chapter 4

Exercise 4.1a

Paragraph 1: 4, 3, 1, 5, 2
Paragraph 2: 4, 2, 1, 5, 3

Exercise 4.1b

1. across
2. above
3. between
4. middle
5. near

Exercise 4.3a

Answers will vary.
1. (given)
2. Contrast: In the past, many mothers did not work outside the home, and the divorce rate was much lower than it is today.
3. Contrast: Reading to children and spending time with them has a much more positive effect than "TV babysitting."
4. Comparison: Adults are influenced by the media, so it is no wonder that children are, too.
5. Comparison: At the same time, the school also has a responsibility.
6. Comparison: Just as babies repeat what they hear when they are learning to talk, as they get older, they imitate the things that they see adults do.

Chapter 5

Exercise 5.1a

Answers will vary. Suggested answers:
1. (given)
2. *Conflict*: Elena realizes that Rose has an eating disorder. She wants her to get help. When Rose refuses, Elena tells Rose's mother. This makes Rose angry, and she tells Elena that she no longer wants to be friends with her.
   Main Point: Being a good friend sometimes means risking a relationship in order to help another person. Even if Rose didn't want to be her friend any more, Elena wanted Rose to be healthy and alive.
3. *Conflict*: Mrs. Paranjpe doesn't want to tell her mother that the older woman is dying. Mr. Paranjpe believes that she should be told so that she can decide how she wants to spend her remaining time.
   Main Point: A person can't always protect a loved one. People have the right to be informed about their medical condition so they can make their own decisions.

Exercise 5.2

Answers will vary. Suggested answers:
1. (given)
2. Many young people begin because they are introduced to drugs by friends.
   Some people start to take drugs out of curiosity or boredom.
   Drug taking is often a gesture of defiance against authority.
   Reasons for deletions: All of these details relate to why people start taking drugs. They have nothing to do with the social effects of drug abuse.

3. Thousands of beautiful designs to choose from.
   People have been tattooing and otherwise decorating their bodies since the first humans began living together in communities.
   Reasons for deletions: The first detail contradicts the idea of "the worst decision I ever made" and is irrelevant. The second detail provides historical background and has nothing to do with making a bad decision to get a tattoo.

Chapter 6

Exercise 6.1a

Answers will vary. Sample answers.

1. Logical and space order development
   I. Air
      A. Dark and dingy
      C. Smells of liquor
      D. Sharp, burning smoke—hard to breathe
   II. Furnishings
      A. Cracked linoleum floor
      B. Cluttered with litter
      C. No athletic equipment or sports—not even a pool table!
      D. Why video games to attract kids
      E. No fire exit
   III. What people are doing there
      A. People nodding out may be on drugs
      B. Bartender—not interested in kids
      C. Two kids drinking beer in the corner

2. Order of importance

   I. Bright, clean rooms
      A. Yellow walls with green trim
      B. Vase of orange African daisies in the waiting room
      C. Toys for kids in the waiting room
      D. New equipment in the examining room
   II. Important information freely available

   A. Wall poster describing safe sex
   B. Booklets on IV drugs and needle exchange programs
III. Respect for you as a person
   A. Not a long wait
   B. Can bring your boyfriend or girl friend along
   C. Can weigh yourself privately
   D. Boxes of condoms easily available
IV. Genuinely concerned staff
   A. Nurse polite, smiling
   B. Nurse told me to take my time with the form
   C. Doctor talks about sex, even if you are too embarrassed to ask

Exercise 6.2b

Answers will vary. Sample answers.

1. Topic My mother's best friend
   I. Her looks
      A. Short and a little chubby
      B. Dyed red hair, short and curly
      C. Wears tight leggings and long shirts
   II. Her voice
      A. Always shouting at her kids
   III. How she acts with me
      A. Kisses and hugs me all the time
      B. I can always tell her my problems

2. Topic In a city park after dark

   I. Sun setting on an autumn evening
      A. Darkness comes on suddenly
      B. Leaves overhead block the receding light
   II. Smells
      A. Odor of garbage from cans rises sharply
      B. Clammy breezes get stronger
   III. What the park sounds like
      A. Ominous crack of twigs underfoot
      B. Scurrying—animals or people?
      C. Screeching of birds
   IV. What you can see—and what you can't
      A. Trees shadows grow grotesque
      B. Rocks and boulders loom large and dark
      C. Pathway out is barely lighted

Chapter 7

Exercise 7.1a

<u>People keep asking me about this.</u> <u>So I decided to write a memo, even though all this information is in the Employee Handbook.</u>
To file a claim for any kind of dental work except a routine exam, X-rays, and cleaning, you must first apply for approval for the procedure. <u>I find this very frustrating, but that's life.</u>
The approval forms are on a clearly marked shelf in my office. Take a form and have your dentist fill it out and send it to the insurer. The address is on the form. When the dentist gets the approval, you can go ahead with the procedure.
<u>I have done this myself, and it does actually work.</u> <u>Good luck!</u>

Exercise 7.1b

1. Format: Personal business letter
2. Format: Memo
3. Format: Personal business letter (or, with school's permission, business letter on school stationery)
4. Format: Business letter
5. Format: Memo

Exercise 7.1c

Answers will vary. Memos should include a memo heading, an opening statement or paragraph, one or more supporting body paragraphs, and a conclusion.
Facts to include:
1. b, c, d, e, f, g, h
2. a, c, d, e, f

Exercise 7.1d

Answers will vary.
1. Letter 1 should include facts a, b, c, d, e, and f. As a personal business letter it should include your own return address above the date. The address of the Social Security Administration office in your area can be found in the blue pages of your telephone directory.
2. Letter 2 should include facts a, c, d, e, g, h, and i. As a business letter it should include a

return address (of the video studio you invented) and an inside address (of the community center you invented).

Exercise 7.2

Answers will vary.
1. Letter 1 should follow the personal business format and include your return address and telephone number and an inside address for the electrician. Suggested logical order of information: h, b, d, a, e, f, g. (Statement c is irrelevant.)
2. Letter 2 should be a personal letter and may or may not include your return address and an inside address for your friend. Suggested process order of directions: c, d, e, b, f, g. (Statement a is irrelevant.)
3. Letter 3 should follow the personal business format and include your return address and telephone number and an inside address for the mechanic. Suggested logical order of information: c, d, e, f, b, h. (Statements a and g are irrelevant.)

Chapter 8

Exercise 8.1a

Answers will vary. Sample answers:
1. Pro: People who are suffering and will die soon anyway should be allowed to choose to die.
   Con: We can never know for sure whether a person will recover for what doctors feel is a terminal illness.
2. Pro: As the high achievement in all-girls schools shows, going to a segregated school can improve your education.
   Con: As the Supreme Court said, schools that are segregated by race cannot give an equal education to all.
3. Pro: The government has the responsibility to provide free hospital care to people who are too poor to pay for it.
   Con: If the government pays for medical care, everyone's taxes will greatly increase.

4. Pro: Research on animals has given us some amazing cures for diseases that we would not be able to get any other way.

   Con: Animals are living, feeling creatures, and they should not be harmed or used just for our benefit.

Exercise 8.1b

Answers will vary. Sample answers:

1. Opinion: Federal funding for the arts makes it possible for children in city shelters to enjoy and learn about theater.

   Request: We need to get together to convince Congress to restore funding for worthwhile arts programs such as these.

2. Opinion: The West Side Center is a great place for kids to go after school.

   Request: Our community needs to raise the money to make sure the West Side Center can remain open.

3. Opinion: Too many innocent people have been gunned down by accident in our neighborhood.

   Request: We need to get the police to arrest drug pushers in our areas and to keep the streets safe.

Exercise 8.2

Answers will vary. Sample answers:

1. Smoking should be banned in all restaurants because it affects the health of restaurant workers and other diners.
2. I love dogs because they make loyal, affectionate pets.
3. Cheating on your income tax is not like stealing because you are not taking money from another person.
4. People should not get divorced because divorce causes children to have behavior and learning problems.
5. Abortion is wrong because the unborn child is a real person with a right to live his or her own life.

Exercise 8.3a

Answers will vary. Sample answers:

1. Deer are living, feeling creatures, and people should not be allowed to kill them just for the fun of it.
2. Children are usually get better care and more attention living with their mother than their father, even if their mother is not a perfect parent.
3. The repair work you did on my car did not fix the problem at all.
4. My son is having trouble learning math with the methods you are using.

Exercise 8.3b

Answers will vary. Sample answers:

1. Dates of your employment at your old job
   Name and address of new employer
   Date that your new job starts
   Your position and duties at your old job
2. Sublet terms of your lease
   Name of your cousin
   Start and end dates of the sublease
   Your cousin's former address
3. Your address and apartment number
   List of specific housing code violations
   Your phone number
   Your landlord's name and phone number
4. Number of young parents in the congregation
   Benefits to parents
   Benefits to children
   Benefits to the congregation

Chapter 9

Exercise 9.1

1. (given)
2. *Topic:* Underline "the rules about who can run for these two bodies and how long a person serves in a single term."
   Question: In what ways do the rules about running and serving in the Senate and the House of Representatives affect how these bodies work?

Instructions: The essay should describe the differences in the Senate and House rules and should contrast how these differences affect the way that the Senate and the House operate.

3. *Topic*: Underline "positive effects of recycling" and/or "how recycling everyday products can benefit our world."
Question: How can recycling benefit our world?
Instructions: The essay should be two to three paragraphs long and should talk about the influence of recycling on our world.

4. *Topic*: Underline "reasons for returning to school" and "problems reaching their educational goals."
Question: What reasons does the person have for returning to school, and what problems does he or she face?
Instructions: The essay should be three or four paragraphs long. It should discuss the reasons and the problem. It should include an opinion about the person's prospects for success as well as reasons for that opinion.

5. *Topic*: Underline "a person you admire."
Question: Why do you admire this person, and what can people learn from his or her good example?
Instructions: The essay should be four paragraphs long. It should include an introductory paragraph that identifies the person and describes the person's good qualities and actions. It should end with a paragraph that summarizes your reasons for admiring this person and states what can be learned from this person.

Chapter 10

Exercise 10.2a

1. (given)
2. OK
3. **X** The sentences about housekeeping and about baking and selling cakes should be crossed out.

Exercise 10.2b

1. (given)
2. (Logical order) 1, 3, 2, 4, 5
3. (Time order) 1, 2, 4, 6, 3, 5

Exercise 10.2c

1. (given)
2. No, the paragraph does not give the day or time of the shower. Some people might also think that the reader should be told how much money he or she is expected to chip in.
3. Yes.

Exercise 10.2d

1. (given)
2. Idea: The course will make the employee better at the job.
Emphasis: No. The writer *did* state the idea twice and made it the last point in the paragraph, but he or she should have included more information about how the course would make him or her a better employee and less information about why it would not interfere with the job.
3. Idea: That having baggers would make the checkout lines move more quickly.
Emphasis: No, the writer has not stated this idea, although it is implied in the paragraph.

Exercise 10.3

Answers may vary. Sample answers:
1. (given)
2. complain
3. unpleasant
4. throb
5. friendlier

Exercise 10.4a

1. (given)
2. Cross out *In my opinion* or *I think*.
3. Cross out *Modern* or *of today*.
4. Cross out *Morning* or *before noon*.
5. Cross out *As a rule* or *always*.

6. Cross out *To my ears.* Also cross out either *still* or *anyway.*

Exercise 10.4b

1. (given)
2. Revision should eliminate the repetition of <u>like</u> and <u>nice</u>.
3. Revision should eliminate the repetition of <u>took</u>.

Chapter 11

Exercise 11.1

Answers will vary. Suggested answers.

1. As you requested, I met with the order fulfillment staff to discuss our recent problem with back orders. We reviewed the backlog records for the past eight weeks.
2. Correct.
3. This is about 35 more per week than usual.
4. (and 5.) We found two specific reasons for this problem. First, one staff member was assigned temporary duty in the Inventory Department due to an emergency.
6. Second, orders overall have increased by about 10 percent. The sales office says Christmas orders are coming in earlier than usual.

Exercise 11.2a

Dear Customer:

Armstrong Manufacturing is delighted that you have ~~had~~ placed your order for Christmas packaging before the rush. This means ~~mean~~ that you are expecting a busy season, which is ~~are~~ good for everyone. We want ~~wants~~ to let you know that your order is ~~are~~ being processed. Due to the large number of early orders we have received ~~receive~~ this year, our fulfillment time has ~~have~~ increased slightly.

This letter is to assure you that your order will ~~have been~~ be processed within the next five days.

Exercise 11.2b

1. she, her
2. me, you, we
3. you, your
4. they
5. We

Exercise 11.2c

1. poorly
2. traditional, prettier
4. low
5. special
6. best

Exercise 11.3

TO: Order Fulfillment <u>Clerks</u>
FROM: Otis Franklin, Director, <u>Order Fulfillment</u>
DATE: November 12, 199-
SUBJECT: Cleaning Up <u>the</u> Order Backlog

Thank you for your cooperation with <u>Tamiko</u> in Ms. McGraw's absence. <u>Her</u> report has helped me find some <u>solutions</u> to the backlog problem. As of <u>November</u> 15, <u>I</u> will be adding a new <u>inventory clerk</u> to the staff of the Inventory Department. Temporarily<u>,</u> until the end of the Christmas <u>season,</u> this person will work in the Order Fulfillment Department. I will be asking <u>Tamiko</u> to take charge of training the new employee<u>.</u>

Until December 22, <u>your department</u> will work overtime on <u>Mondays, Wednesdays,</u> and Fridays. <u>A</u> schedule will be posted on the bulletin board. Please let me know if unplanned overtime will be a problem for any of you<u>.</u>

Glossary

abusing (uh-BYOOZ-ihng) *verb* Using wrongly or improperly.

addiction (uh-DIHK-shuhn) *noun* The condition of being dependent on a habit-forming substance.

administrative assistant (ad-MIHN-uh-strayt-ihv uh-SIHS-tuhnt) *noun* A person whose job it is to do office work for an executive, such as typing, filing, and scheduling.

AIDS (aydz) *noun* Abbreviation for *acquired immune deficiency syndrome* (uh-KWEYERD ih-MYOON dih-FIH-shuhn-see SIHN-drohm). A deadly disease that destroys the body's ability to protect itself from illnesses. AIDS is spread from person to person by blood, semen, and other body fluids.

alcoholic (al-kuh-HAWL-ihk) *noun* A person suffering from excessive and habitual consumption of alcohol.

analysis (uh-NAL-ih-sihs) *noun* A study of a problem to determine its cause.

analyze (AN-uh-leyez) *verb* To examine the different aspects of a topic. To break an idea into its parts.

atmosphere (AT-muh-sfihr) *noun* The mood or feeling of a place.

audience (AWD-ee-uhns) *noun* Listeners, viewers, or readers.

authority (uh-THOR-uh-tee) *noun* Someone who is an expert on a particular topic.

backlog (BAK-lawg) *noun* Work that has not been performed or material that has not been processed.

body paragraph (BAH-dee PAR-uh-graf) *noun* A paragraph in an esssay that develops one idea supporting the thesis statement.

brainstorm (BRAYN-stawrm) *verb* To randomly list ideas about a subject as they flow freely from your mind.

brand name (brand naym) *noun* A registered product name used by its sellers to identify and promote it to the public.

budget (BUH-juht) *noun* A system for planning the amount of money to be spent for a period of time, based on income and expenses.

bullet (BOOL-iht) *noun* A large black dot printed before an item in a list to call attention to the item.

campaign (kam-PAYN) *noun* A connected series of activities designed to cause a particular result. In an election campaign, the campaigner works to become elected to office.

cause (kawz) *noun* A force or event that makes something happen.

character (KAR-ihk-tuhr) noun A person in a story.

citizen (SIHT-uh-zuhn) *noun* A person who owes allegiance to a country and deserves to be protected by it. A citizen may be native-born or naturalized.

City Council (SIHT-ee KOWN-suhl) *noun* The part of a city's government that makes the laws for the city.

climax (KLEYE-maks) *noun* The most exciting part of the plot of a story when the conflict is resolved.

cluster map (KLUH-ster mahp) *noun* A visual drawing of ideas using circles and lines to connect ideas that are related to each other.

compare (kuhm-PAIR) *verb* To point out similarities.

comparison shopping (kuhm-PAIR-ih-suhn SHAHP-pihng) *verb* Going from store to store or in some other way comparing goods and prices before making a purchase.

completeness (kuhm-PLEET-nehs) *noun* The characteristic of including all necessary information.

conclusion (kuhn-KLOO-zhuhn) *noun* The ending of a written piece that restates the thesis, ties the ideas together, and leaves the reader with a parting thought.

condolence (kuhn-DOH-luhnts) *noun* An expression of sympathy, especially for a death.

condom (KAHN-duhm) *noun* A covering for the penis used to prevent pregnancy during sex. Latex (rubber) condoms also help protect against AIDS and other diseases.

conflict (KAHN-flihkt) *noun* A problem that a character in a story must solve.

Congress (KAHN-gruhs) *noun* The highest law-making body of the United States. Congress is made up of the Senate and the House of Representatives.

contrast (kuhn-TRAST) *verb* To point out differences.

cover letter (KUV-uhr LEHT-uhr) *noun* The letter a job hunter sends with a resume.

dangling modifier (DAN-glihng MAHD-uh-feye-uhr) *noun* A modifier that is not logically attached to any word.

dependence (duh-PEHN-dehns) *noun* Being influenced or controlled by something; drug addiction.

depressed (dih-PREHST) *adjective* Low in spirits.

descriptive (dih-SKRIHP-tihv) *adjective* Expressing the content or feelings of observations or experiences.

descriptive purpose (dih-SKRIHP-tihv PER-puhs) *noun* A purpose for writing that aims to describe someone or something.

dialogue (DEYE-uh-lawg) *noun* Conversation between several characters in a story.

dictionary (DIHK-shuh-ner-ee) *noun* A reference book of alphabetized words. Each entry shows word pronunciation, meaning, and other information.

drafting (DRAFT-ihng) (1) *noun* The stage in the writing process of getting ideas down quickly and completely. (2) *verb* The act of writing.

dry cleaning (dreye KLEEN-ing) *noun* A process of cleaning clothing using chemicals and no water.

editing (EHD-uht-ihng) (1) *noun* The stage in the writing process of checking for errors in spelling,

capitalization, and grammar. (2) *verb* The act of rewriting or revising written work.

editorial (ehd-uh-TOHR-ee-uhl) *noun* A newspaper or magazine article that gives the opinion of the editor or publisher.

effect (ih-FEHKT) *noun* A result.

emphasis (EHM-fuh-suhs) *noun* The stress given to an important idea.

energy (EHN-uhr-jee) *noun* Resources used to produce power to do work.

Environmental Protection Department (ihn-veye-ruhn-MEHNT-uhl pruh-TEHK-shuhn dih-PAHRT-muhnt) *noun* The part of a city or state government that regulates activities affecting the air, water, and soil.

essay (EH-say) *noun* A written composition that provides information and often expresses a point of view.

essay question (EH-say KWEHS-chuhn) *noun* A test question that asks the test taker to write an essay, usually a few paragraphs long.

evidence (EHV-uh-duhns) *noun* Proof; something that shows the truth of a statement.

expert (EHK-spuhrt) *noun* Someone who has a great deal of knowledge in a particular field.

fad (fad) *noun* A quickly passing style or pastime.

First Amendment (fuhrst uh-MEHND-muhnt) *noun* One of the ten amendments to the United States Constitution, known together as the Bill of Rights. The First Amendment guarantees freedom of religion, freedom of speech, freedom of the press, freedom of assembly (getting together in a group), and freedom to petition the government.

fraud (frawd) *noun* Cheating by trickery.

generic brand (juh-NEHR-ihk brand) *noun* A general name associated with a store name; often thought to be of lower quality than brand name products.

government (GUHV-uhr-muhnt) *noun* The collection of leaders, law-makers, and judges that together create public policy and are responsible for law and order in a society.

HIV-positive (AYCH-EYE-VEE PAH-zuh-tihv) *adjective* Infected with HIV, the virus that causes AIDS. HIV is the abbreviation for *human immunodeficiency virus* (HYOO-muhn IH-myoo-noh-dih-FIH-shuhn-see VEYE-ruhs).

House of Representatives (hows uhv rehp-rih-ZEHN-tuh-tihvz) *noun* The lower house of the U.S. Congress.

immunization shots (ihm-yuh-neye-ZAY-shuhn shahts) *noun* Injections that prevent children from getting diseases.

impartial (ihm-PAHR-shuhl) *adjective* Neutral; having no particular bias or prejudice.

impulse buying (IHM-puhls BEYE-ihng) *verb* The act of making purchases without planning ahead or thinking of the consequences.

incident (IHN-suh-duhnt) *noun* A situation or an event.

informative purpose (ihn-FAWR-muh-tihv PER-puhs) *noun* A purpose for writing that aims to explain how or why something happens.

intended outcome (ihn-TEHND-uhd OWT-kuhm) *noun* The effect a writer wants to cause in the reader. This outcome may be a feeling or an action.

interpret (ihn-TER-preht) *verb* To explain the meaning.

introduction (ihn-truh-DUHK-shuhn) *noun* The opening statement or paragraph in a written piece that explains the thesis to the reader.

introductory paragraph (ihn-truh-DUHK-tuh-ree PAR-uh-graf) *noun* A paragraph that contains a general statement, a thesis statement, and sentences that explain the writer's purpose or point of view.

irrelevant (ihr-EHL-uh-vuhnt) *adjective* Not related to a topic or purpose.

IV drugs (EYE-VEE druhgz) *noun* Abbreviation for *intravenous* (ihn-truh-VEE-nuhs) drugs. Illegal drugs, such as heroin, that are injected into the veins with a needle, or syringe (suh-RINJ).

jittery (JIHT-uh-ree) *adjective* Uneasy; nervous.

landfill (LAND-fihl) *noun* A place used for burying garbage and rubbish under a layer of earth.

letter of request (LEHT-uhr uhv rih-KWEHST) *noun* A letter that asks for information or asks the reader to perform an action.

letter to the editor (LEH-tuhr too thuh EHD-duht-uhr) *noun* A letter written to a newspaper or magazine in order to express an opinion or give information.

letterhead (LEHT-uhr-hehd) *noun* Stationery that has a printed heading, usually giving the name, address, and telephone numbers of a business or an organization.

logical order (LAHJ-ih-kuhl AWRD-uhr) *noun* The writing technique of organizing details according to how they are related to each other and to the main idea.

mayor (MAY-uhr) *noun* A person who heads a city, town, or borough.

mechanics (mih-KAN-ihks) *noun* The details of writing that include capitalization, punctuation, and spelling.

memo (MEH-moh) *noun* See *memorandum*.

memorandum (mem-uh-RAHN-duhm) *noun* An informal written communication, within an office, a business, or an organization.

misplaced modifier (mihs-PLAYST MAHD-uh-feye-uhr) *noun* A modifier that is attached to the wrong word.

narrative purpose (NAR-uh-tihv PER-puhs) *noun* A purpose for writing that aims to tell a story or relate a sequence of events.

natural resource (NACH-uh-ruhl REE-sawrs) *noun* Something found in nature that is useful to people.

needle exchange program (NEE-duhl eks-CHAYNJ PROH-gram) *noun* Government-approved plans that allow drug abusers to get sterile needles (syringes) when they give up used ones. Sharing used needles is a major way to transmit AIDS, infection, and other diseases.

newsletter (NOOZ-leh-tuhr) *noun* A small publication that gives news and information of interest to a particular group.

objective (uhb-JEHK-tihv) *adjective* Unbiased; unprejudiced; neutral; factual.

op-ed page (ahp-ehd payj) *noun* A page in a newspaper, usually opposite the editorials, that contains columns, opinion articles, political cartoons, and other special features.

opinion (uh-PIHN-yuhn) *noun* A view, judgment, bias, or belief held by a person about a particular matter.

order (AWRD-uhr) *noun* The characteristic of having a logical sequence.

order fulfillment (AWRD-uhr fuhl-FIHL-mehnt) *noun* The shipment of products to customers who have purchased them.

outline (OWT-leyen) *noun* An organized list of ideas that shows how ideas are related to each other.

overpriced (OH-ver-preyesd) *adjective* Charging more for goods or services than their real value.

pace (pays) *noun* Rate of progress.

paragraph (PAR-uh-graf) *noun* One or more sentences on a related topic.

Parent-Teachers Association (PTA) (PAHR-uhnt TEE-chuhrz uh-soh-see-AY-shun) *noun* An organization made up of teachers at a particular school and the parents whose children attend the school. The purpose of a PTA is to support and improve the school.

parenting education (PAR-uhnt-ihng ehj-yuh-KAY-shuhn) *noun* Programs that teach parenting skills.

performance appraisal (per-FAWR-muhns uh-PRAY-zuhl) *noun* The evaluation of an employee's work.

persuasive purpose (per-SWAY-sihv PER-puhs) *adjective* A purpose for writing that aims to convince or influence another person's actions or beliefs.

picket line (PIHK-uht leyen) *noun* A line of people in a demonstration or protest; a line of workers on strike.

plot (plaht) *noun* A series of related events that make up the action of a story.

political action committee (puh-LIHT-ih-kuhl AK-shuhn kuh-MIHT-ee) *noun* A group formed to raise and give money to candidates likely to support the group's interest. The abbreviation is PAC (pak).

poll (pohl) *noun* A place where people vote.

portfolio (port-FOH-lee-oh) *noun* A collection of written work and reference material often kept in a notebook or folder.

prewriting (PREE-reyet-ihng) (1) *noun* The stage in the writing process of collecting and organizing ideas according to a purpose. (2) *verb* The act of preparation for writing.

process order (PRAH-sehs AWRD-uhr) *noun* The writing technique of organizing the steps in a task in sequence.

proofreading (PROOF-ree-dihng) *noun* The slow and careful reading of revised work and marking errors for correction.

proofreading symbols (PROOF-ree-dihng SIHM-buhlz) *noun* Marks used by professional editors and writers to show correction of errors in written material.

publishing (PUB-lihsh-ihng) (1) *noun* The stage in the writing process of sharing a piece of writing with others. (2) *verb* The act of distributing a written work to others.

purpose (PER-puhs) *noun* The general reason for writing: descriptive, informative, narrative, persuasive. Also see: *intended outcome*.

qualifications (kwahl-uh-fuh-KAY-shuhnz) *noun* The skills, training, experience, and education that fits a person for a job.

quality (KWAL-uh-tee) *adjective* The level of value or degree of excellence of goods or services.

recycling (ree-SEYE-kuhl-ihng) *verb* Processing waste materials to be used again.

register (REHJ-uh-stuhr) *verb* To enroll in order to vote in elections.

relevant (REHL-uh-vuhnt) *adjective* Related to a topic or purpose.

report (rih-PAWRT) *noun* A lengthy piece of informative writing that usually gives statistics or other factual information about a particular topic. Reports follow a standard format and usually involve researching (investigating) the topic.

representative (rehp-rih-ZEHNT-uh-tihv) *noun* A member of the United States House of Representatives in Congress or a member of a state legislature. United States representatives are elected by voters in a specific district. Their job is to make laws.

responsibility (rih-spahn-suh-BIHL-uh-tee) *noun* A task or burden assigned to someone.

resume (REHZ-uh-may) *noun* A document that summarizes a job hunter's qualifications.

retail (REE-tayl) *noun* The selling of goods directly to the people who will use them.

returns (rih-TEHRNZ) *noun plural* Merchandise returned to a store for exchange, credit, or refund.

revising (rih-VEYEZ-ihng) (1) *noun* The stage in the writing process that serves to reorganize, rewrite, and improve a document. (2) *verb* The act of rewriting or improving a written work.

revision (rih-VIHZH-uhn) *noun* (1) The act of improving a piece of writing. (2) A revised piece of writing.

rough draft (ruhf draft) *noun* The first written version of a complete piece.

run (run) *verb* To release color, as some dyed fabrics.

safe sex (sayf sehks) *noun* Practices, primarily use of condoms, that prevent body fluids, such as blood and semen, from passing from one partner to another during sex. Safe sex makes it much less likely that one partner will infect the other with AIDS or other diseases.

salesmanship (SAYLZ-muhn-shihp) *noun* The ability to sell.

school board (skool bawrd) *noun* A group of people, usually elected, who run the schools in a particular district.

seam (seem) *noun* A joint between two pieces of fabric or material, often sewn in place.

Senate (SEHN-uht) *noun* The upper house of the U.S. Congress.

senator (SEHN-uh-tuhr) *noun* A member of the United States Senate in Congress or a member of a state legislature. Two United States senators are elected from each state. Their job is to make laws.

setting (SEHT-ihng) *noun* Where and when the action of a story takes place.

sewage treatment plant (SOO-ihj TREET-muhnt plant) *noun* A building where the waste matter from sewers is processed before it is released into the environment.

sexually transmitted disease (STD) (SEHK-shoo-lee tranz-MIHT-uhd duh-ZEEZ) *noun* An infection caused by bacteria or viruses that are spread from one person to another through sexual contact.

sibling (SIHB-lihng) *noun* A brother or sister.

social drinker (SOH-shuhl DRIHNK-er) *noun* A person who consumes alcoholic drinks while at a party or another gathering with friends.

source (sohrs) *noun* A publication or other reference given to a reader to show where factual information came from.

space order (spays AWRD-uhr) *noun* Organization showing relationships of things according to location.

stages of development (STAJ-uhz uhv dih-VEHL-uhp-muhnt) *noun* The physical and mental growth of a child based on the child's age.

state legislature (stayt LEHJ-uh-slay-chuhr) *noun* The highest law making body in a particular state. Its members are elected by the people of the state.

state insurance commission (stayt ihn-SHOOR-uhns kuh-MIH-shuhn) *noun* The agency of a state's government that oversees and regulates insurance companies in the state.

statement of purpose (STAYT-muhnt uhv PER-puhs) *noun* A sentence or two that gives the topic, purpose, audience, and intended outcome of a piece of writing.

statistics (stuh-TIHS-tihks) *noun* Numerical facts. Complex or difficult numerical facts are usually brought together and discussed by an expert called a *statistician* (sta-tuh-STIH-shuhn).

story map (STAWR-ee map) *noun* A graphic diagram of narrative elements.

subjective (suhb-JEHK-tihv) *adjective* Personal; having or expressing a particular feeling or belief.

summary (SUM-uh-ree) *noun* A brief retelling of the main points of an essay or other piece of writing.

synonym (SIHN-uh-nihm) *noun* A word that means the same, or almost the same, as another word.

synthetic (sihn-THEHT-ihk) *adjective* Made by people from different ingredients. Not natural.

taxpayer (TAKS-pay-uhr) *noun* A person who must pay tax to a local, state, or federal government. You do not have to be a citizen in order to be a taxpayer.

temper tantrum (TEHM-puhr TAN-truhm) *noun* A display of anger, usually consisting of loud screaming, crying, and thrashing about.

thesaurus (thih-SAWR-uhs) *noun* A book of words and their synonyms, also including phrases and expressions that have similar meanings.

thesis statement (THEE-sis STAYT-mehnt) *noun* A sentence that summarizes the topic; the position or point of view that will be developed in a written piece.

thesis (THEE-sis) *noun* A summary of a topic. A reason for writing.

thrifty (THRIHF-tee) *adjective* Careful about spending money.

time order (teyem AWRD-uhr) *noun* Organization showing events in the order they occurred.

topic (TAHP-ihk) *noun* The subject of a paragraph or a longer piece of writing.

topic sentence (TAHP-ihk SEHN-tuhns) *noun* A complete thought that expresses the main idea of a paragraph or a longer piece of writing.

transition (TRANS-ih-shuhn) *noun* A link between ideas.

unity (YOO-nuh-tee) *noun* The effect created when all the parts of a paragraph work together.

want ads (wahnt adz) *noun* Advertisements for jobs available.

wardrobe (WAWR-drohb) *noun* The entire set of clothing that you own.

wordiness (WERD-ee-nehs) *noun* The quality of taking more words than necessary to say something.

workmanship (WEHRK-muhn-shihp) *noun* The way a product's materials have been shaped, formed, or put together. Some warranties promise that the product's *workmanship* was not defective.

writing plan (REYET-ihng plan) *noun* A plan written before a first draft, including topic, purpose, audience, style, intended outcomes, and an outline of ideas and supporting details.

writing process (REYET-ihng PRAH-sehs) *noun* A series of five steps that lead to a finished written work: *prewriting, drafting, revising, editing,* and *publishing.*